GUIDE TO
OLD HAVANA

Original idea, text and photographs © Com-Relieve, S.A.
Title of collection and layout © Editorial Escudo de Oro, S.A.

3rd Edition

I.S.B.N. 84-378-1958-X

Com-Relieve, S.A.
Editorial Escudo de Oro, S.A.

Printed in EEC by
FISA-ESCUDO DE ORO, S.A.

Dep. Legal B. 26138-1999

Antique fans in Plaza de Armas.

WALKING IN HAVANA

You get to know a city from its streets, by walking among its people. Old Havana opens up to those who live it on foot.

Time here does not seem to move so quickly as in other places, but it is certain that in few cities is each instant so intense, nor do simple things take on quite such a sublime dimension as in Havana. This is due to the city's most valuable possession - its inhabitants. The inhabitants of Havana are exuberant in love and hyperbolic in their emotions. Everyone is their friend and they are everyone's friend… There are no strangers in Havana, since newcomers soon form part of the large family. They realise that they belong to this family when they find themselves talking to a Havanan for hours, someone they had never known before and who they will probably never see again, as if they had known them all their life. Havana is a singular confessional where the Havanan willingly ordains himself the priest of laughter, saving souls from the most serious depressions.

Extrovert, the people of Havana bear with decorum the economic difficulties which befell the country during the nineties, and which will be no secret to you when you start to walk through the streets. On your way you will see more than one queue to buy food, buses full of passengers or hundreds of cyclists instead of luxury cars, all forming part of a culture of resistance which performs the miracle of the loaves and the fishes every day...Everybody eats, and everybody lives, and each person knows that nobody is alone in this city and this gift is priceless, no gold can pay for it in this world where so many die abandoned yet surrounded by great abundance.

The other thing about Havana is music. The Havanan's biorhythm is always moving to a music sheet. Music is heard in all the streets and occupies all the time and space in the city, sometimes wildly, but mostly as a backdrop to everyday life. Silence is a luxury in Havana and is nearly always an aberration of the senses.

The sun also shows the quintessence of Havana, revealing virtue and nobility in the relief work of stones and ordinary bricks. The city's buildings are its history, wrought and told by the infinite columns, the imposing entrances and arcades and multicoloured glasses.

This guide to La Habana Vieja -Old Havana- is an attempt to share our love for this warm city where we live. We have designed six itineraries to take you by the hand through its streets and squares. They are for the active visitor, always on the move and with an inexhaustible capacity for wonder and discovery.

Picturesque characters of the Calle Obispo.

Calle Leonor Pérez.

The first itinerary takes us to open spaces and avenues, with various urban landscapes limited by the Prado, the sea, the shopping area and the National Capitol. The second itinerary goes to the old walls and churches, taking us also to the quays and the most typical streets in Havana. The third focuses on Plaza San Francisco and the Plaza Vieja, with a walk around the museums and grand old houses which were the foundations of colonial architecture. It ends with the climb to the Cristo de Havana. The fourth itinerary takes us to the oldest part of the town, the Plaza de Armas and the Cathedral. The fifth itinerary takes in the historical scenarios of the revolutionary struggle, testified by the Granma Memorial, the Museum of the Revolution and Martyrs' Park on the La Punta esplanade. The sixth and last itinerary takes in the historical and military Morro-Cabaña complex, with its imposing fortresses and extraordinary views.

Each itinerary has its own map. You will thus follow a coherent route and easily find the objectives of interest to you.

In summer the most suitable times to walk in Havana are the early morning and the early evening, with light, loose clothing and comfortable shoes. In winter any time is good, as the average temperature is very pleasant.

At the end of the guide we add a directory of hotels, restaurants and shops to be found in Old Havana. There is also a list of useful telephone numbers.

Old Havana is a very peaceful area given special protection by the forces of law and order. You can approach them for any type of help. In fact anyone will help you, as the typical Havanan has a strong sense of solidarity and good manners.

Public toilets are generally to be found in public buildings and hotels. The hotel tourist bureaux offer all useful information, as well as first aid at their medical posts.

The San Cristóbal Agency of the Compañía Habaguanex S.A., specialises in tourism in Old Havana and is to be found in Plaza San Francisco in Calle Oficios between Teniente Rey and Amargura. Here you may request all types of services to make your visit to the city more agreeable.

Cuban cigars.

Plaza del Cristo (18th-19th century).

THE OLD HISTORY OF OLD HAVANA:

The city of Havana's origins are shrouded in mystery. There are no papers or documents to witness the details of its founding, lost in the transformations of time and the blazing torches of pirates.

However, we know from the disperse testimonies of the so-called chroniclers of the Indies that it was not originally where it is now, but 50 km south, probably by the mouth of the river Mayabeque, called Onicajinal by the Indians.

The chronicles tell that Pánfilo de Narváez, a fierce, ruthless Conquistador, founded it on 25 July 1514 with the name San Cristóbal, since it was the saint's day and also in honour of the Great Admiral who discovered America. Havana came from the Indians, who gave this name to the lands belonging to the local chief Habaguanex.

The town did not last long in the south, as its inhabitants were tormented by plagues of insects and the mires of the low lands. The river Almendares in the north was not suitable either, but rather Puerto de Carenas, extensive and magnificent and with a benign climate, discovered by Sebastián de Ocampo, who took refuge there in 1508 while he was circumnavigating to ascertain whether Cuba was a continent or an island.

So, when the Council held its first mass and meeting on 16 November 1519 the foundation of San Cristóbal of Havana became a material and legal fact.

The town was very modest in the beginning, and was no more than a poor hamlet of shacks made of wood and guano surrounding a little square from which sprouted the first streets, Calles Oficios and Mercaderes, symbols of the stamp which would forever mark its future destiny, work and business.

Port of call for globetrotters, conquistadors and adventurers, San Cristóbal de la Habana earned mettle and fame as the key to the New World. The port was usually host to between 19 and 30 ships greedy to fleece Moctezuma and gorged on their return with holds full of the gold of the defeated gods.

In 1537 pirates came to raze, kill and burn in Havana. This was the tone of events in the 16th and 17th centuries. The greatest disaster was caused by Jackes de Sores, the French Corsair, in 1555.

He destroyed the wretched fortress which defended the town, taking it and many prisoners. He asked for 30 thousand pesos ransom and 100 cargoes of cassava. He made a pact with the Governor, who reneged and attacked the pirates by night. The indignant privateer cut the captives' throats and destroyed everything to be found for leagues around.

Like the Phoenix the hapless and desolate town rose again with new strength, this time made of stone and with well prepared cannons. El Morro became a watchtower of light and rocks at the entrance of the bay, with the fire power of the Doce Apóstoles

The Bay of Havana (19th century).

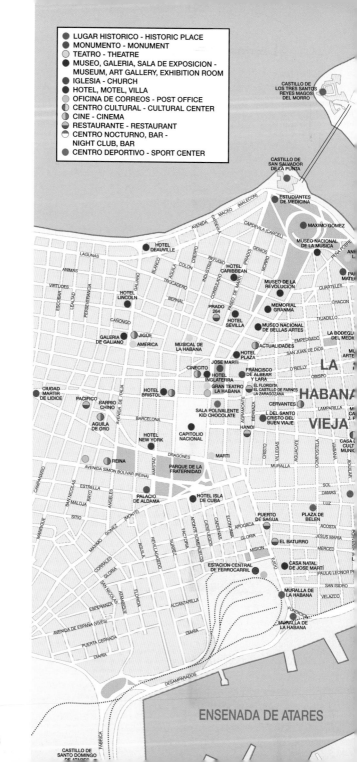

LUGAR HISTORICO - HISTORIC PLACE
MONUMENTO - MONUMENT
TEATRO - THEATRE
MUSEO, GALERIA, SALA DE EXPOSICION -
MUSEUM, ART GALLERY, EXHIBITION ROOM
IGLESIA - CHURCH
HOTEL, MOTEL, VILLA
OFICINA DE CORREOS - POST OFFICE
CENTRO CULTURAL - CULTURAL CENTER
CINE - CINEMA
RESTAURANTE - RESTAURANT
CENTRO NOCTURNO, BAR -
NIGHT CLUB, BAR
CENTRO DEPORTIVO - SPORT CENTER

8

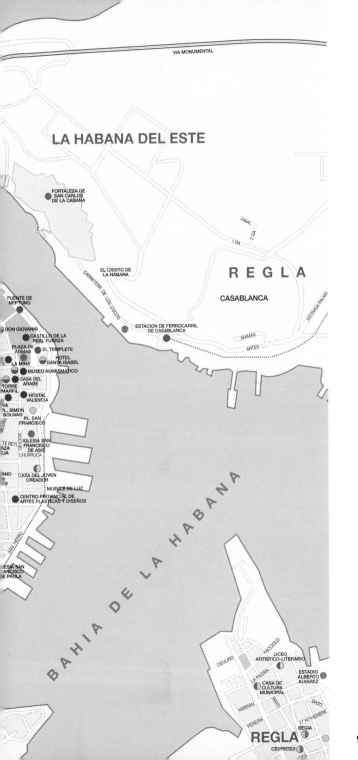

VIA MONUMENTAL

LA HABANA DEL ESTE

FORTALEZA DE
SAN CARLOS
DE LA CABAÑA

FINAL

1 RA

2 DA

R E G L A

EL CRISTO DE
LA HABANA

CARRETERA DE LOS COCOS

CASABLANCA

ESTRADA PALMA

FUENTE DE
NEPTUNO

DON GIOVANNI

CASTILLO DE LA
REAL FUERZA

PLAZA DE
ARMAS

EL TEMPLETE

LA MINA

HOTEL
SANTA ISABEL

ESTACION DE FERROCARRIL
DE CASABLANCA

ANIMAS

ARTES

MUSEO NUMISMATICO

TORRE
MARFIL

CASA DEL
ARABE

HOSTAL
VALENCIA

PL. SIMON
BOLIVAR

PL. SAN
FRANCISCO

TE REYI

JZA
JA

IGLESIA SAN
FRANCISCO
DE ASIS

CHURRUCA

ANO
S

CASA DEL JOVEN
CREADOR

MUELLE DE LUZ

CENTRO PROVINCIAL DE
ARTES PLASTICAS Y DISEÑOS

SAN PEDRO

ESIA SAN
ANCISCO
E PAULA

B A H I A   D E   L A   H A B A N A

FACCIOLO

CEULINO

LA PIEDRA

CASA DE
CULTURA
MUNICIPAL

AMBRAN

MARTI

LICEO
ARTISTICO-LITERARIO

ESTADIO
ALBERTO
ALVAREZ

BAZO

PEREIRA

27 NOVIEMBRE

REGIA

REGLA

CESPEDES

9

Plaza Vieja (18th-19th century).

crossing with that of San Salvador de La Punta to close the way to intruders. The walls which would close the town's perimeter for 200 years were cut in blocks from coastal quarries.

Havana gained in class with the governors who came to settle there and also when King Philip II, in thanks for great services rendered to the Crown by its inhabitants, gave it the status and benefits of a City conferred by the Royal Decree of 16 July 1592.

The town was embellished by splendid houses with patios and fountains built by master builders inspired by the Mudéjar style. They also built façades, porticoes and columns in the baroque style with tropical touches, while the pastoral look became transformed into more urban and Peninsular features, with churches and convents whose domes rose above all that surrounded them.

Spain's European neighbours were always envious of Havana, which was again under threat when two hundred ships, two thousand cannons and more than twenty thousand men besieged the city. At the beginning of summer 1762 the English presented off the coast of the city the most formidable fleet ever seen in the Americas.

The city's defence was compromised by poor decision making. Spanish honour was saved by heroic resistance in the Castle of Los Tres Reyes Del Morro , under the command of ship's Captain Don Luis de Velasco. Guerrilla bands headed by Creoles Pepe

Antonio and Aguiar fought with the English on local roads and in the mountains, using machetes and blunderbusses.

The cannons thundered against the fortress for one and a half months and the British, exhausted by the enervating climate and illness, realised that they could not put off the attack any longer. On 30 July 1762 they blew up one of the bastions and assaulted Velasco's redoubt. In the ensuing battle, Velasco himself fell mortally wounded. The British were made aware of the inhabitants' dislike of them throughout their year of domination. Perhaps the seed of what is today Cuban pride in their nation began to incubate from that time. This is a love for their country above all other things.

Havana was returned to Spain at the treaty of Versailles, or rather to Cuba, to put it better. King Charles III understood that after the English commercial expansion the only feasible way for Havana was to permit the free and prosperous trade already fomented there, in contrast to the previous brutal monopoly.

The lesson learned from the experience of the invasion led to precautions for the future. The defenses at El Morro were restored and extended, and on the previously bare heights the splendid fortresses of La Cabaña, El Príncipe and Atarés were built. Militias were organised and trained, taking all precautions so that there would be no repetition of the experience.

The 18th century ended under the exceptional mandate of the Governor Don Luis de Las Casas, far and away the most gifted head of the Island during the colonial period. Las Casas promoted the economy, education, agriculture and sciences with the support

Bay entrance (19th century).

High relief of the door of the National Capitol with historic motifs.

of the most educated Creoles. He founded the first public library, the newspaper El Periódico de La Habana and the influential Sociedad Económica de Amigos del País. His government presided one of the most prosperous periods known.

The dawning of the 19th century found Havana in constant growth. New avenues and boulevards were to be seen, while the now obsolete city walls were pulled down to make way for new urbanisation projects. The city took over the fertile extramural savanna and extended its blocks south west into it. In the west it overcame the reefs and hilly terrain in El Vedado to build villas and small palaces. Electricity reached Havana in the 19th century, along with the telegraph, the railway, the cinema and the steamship.

There was an uprising in the east of the country in 1868, which marked the beginning of three decades of fighting for independence. Havana also took part, and found its own role in the brawls and political struggles of Creoles and mainland Spanish. The city was a witness to conspiracies, summary executions and the irreverent behaviour of the youths of the Acera del Louvre movement.

The war finished with the century and Spain left forever its last American domain.

The modern era entered the city on North American capital. Old colonial constructions were demolished to make way for other buildings grand in their architectural design and with imposing neoclassical façades. Banks, commercial centres and public administration buildings were inserted, sometimes tastelessly and shamelessly, among the venerable mansions of counts and marquises. Absolute gems of the city of Havana's architectural patrimony were lost forever or altered by wild restoration.

During the sixties the Revolutionary Government instituted a coherent policy to recover the historical ambience of Old Havana. Many buildings have been returned to their previous appearance, due to patient investigation and reconstruction work, with the resulting functional and ambient lease of new life.

One great merit of the project is that is has managed to obtain the enthusiastic collaboration of the inhabitants of Old Havana in the work to recover their habitat as part of creative community action.

Declared World Heritage in 1982 by UNESCO, Old Havana benefits from international recognition of its architecture, town-planning and history.

Its image today foresees a brilliant future of which present inhabitants and those to come may feel proud.

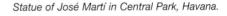

Statue of José Martí in Central Park, Havana.

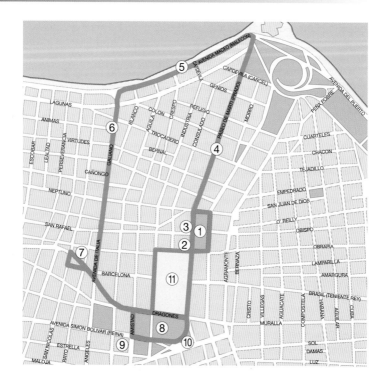

ITINERARY NUMBER ONE:

1- Central Park (Parque Central).
2- Gran Teatro de La Habana.
3- Hotel Inglaterra.
4- Paseo del Prado.
5- El Malecón (the jetty).
6- Avenida Galiano.
7- *Barrio Chino* (Chinese Quarter).
8- Fraternity Park (Parque de la Fraternidad).
9- Palace of Aldama.
10- Fountain of La India.
11- National Capitol.

Due to its privileged position between Old and Modern Havana, there are few places in the city so well situated for the beginning of a walk as the **Central Park (1).** You may go literally anywhere from here, and wherever you are in the city someone will always be able to tell you how to get there. For this reason, and in order to help, various itineraries in this guide begin at the Central Park.

Like most of the architecture in its era, the Central Park and surroundings have a strong neoclassical influence. Its present appearance dates from 1927 when it was completely remodelled as part of the construction project of the nearby National Capitol.

The statue of the Cuban National Hero of Independence, José Martí, is in its centre. This monument, put up on the tenth anniversary of the beginning of the War of 1895, in which Martí's involvement was complete, was the first to be erected at the end of Spanish domination. It was inaugurated on 24 February 1905. The author was the Italian sculptor Giusseppe Neri.

A walk around the park will invariably take us to the most prominent of the buildings surrounding it, the **Gran Teatro de La Habana (2),** also called García Lorca. Its stones and marbles make up a fantasy of arcades, columns, relief work and balconies, crowned by various groups of sculptures. The four small towers capped by winged glories give it a touch of singular architectural personality. The present building dates from 1915, and was constructed by the Sociedad Centro Gallego for its social centre, on the structure of the great functions hall of the Teatro Tacón which had existed since 1838. Respecting the theatre almost in its entirety, the remodelling introduced only a few improvements which embellished it considerably. The Gran Teatro de La Habana holds 2 thousand spectators, and its stage has been trodden by well known luminaries, the most famous being the sopranos Claudia Muzzio and Helena Rakowska,

Central Park.

Gran Teatro de La Habana.

the tragic Adelaida Ristori, Sarah Bernhard, directors Tulio Serafín and Erich Kleiber and the tenor Enrico Caruso who raised the theatre to the heights of glory in 1920, shortly before his death.

Next to the Coliseo, and separated from it by the Bulevar de San Rafael, is the **Hotel Inglaterra (3),** the oldest in the country, whose doors have been open since 1856. Its Patio Sevillano is an essential setting for noble meetings and pleasant group chats, while its Louvre arcades are an invitation slowly to enjoy strong Cuban coffee, as the tradition demands, where before duels were fought over love and patriotism.

Antonio Maceo was a guest there in 1890. An exceptional man of great renown in England, Maceo was one of the greatest Cuban military chiefs of all time, and in 1895 carried off the feat, comparable only with Hannibal crossing the Alps, of bringing the war of independence from the east to the west of the country, fighting Spanish forces which outnumbered him by one hundred to one in terms of men and ammunition. Antonio Maceo, also known as the Bronze Titan, is probably the only soldier in any war to have survived 24 bullet wounds.

In the five months of his stay in Havana this Cuban leader, a living legend and a gentleman, used to walk up the **Paseo del Prado (4),** beginning one hundred metres from the hotel. This is the next point on our route.

For more than two centuries the Prado, now also known as Paseo de Martí in homage to the Apostle, has been one of the most beautiful and crowded avenues, and is much loved by the Havanans. The Marquis of La Torre began construction of the original boulevard in 1772. It went from the Castle of San Salvador de la Punta to Calle Neptuno, exactly where it is today. It was restored and embellished in the 19th century and called the Alameda de Isabel II. For many years it was the aristocratic road par excellence, with sumptuous elegant small palaces on both sides in the time-honoured style of those in Paris, Madrid and Florence. Among the boulevard's unique spectacles were the Carnaval festivities, a true outpouring of happiness, beauty and colour, which have come down to our times as a valuable civic tradition. The bronze lions guarding the entrance to the boulevard are a symbol of an entire nostalgic and romantic era. The Paseo de Martí ends at the statue of Juan Clemente Zenea, the sad poet shot in 1871, and who seems to be wording, inspired by the sea, an interminable sonnet to love and freedom. On the right Martyrs' Park bears witness to those who suffered torment in what was the Tacón prison. Ahead the bastions of San Salvador de la Punta smooth out to afford a view of the hills on the bay. To the left, walking on the concrete wall itself, the city offers us its entire maritime perspective in an impressive panorama.

Construction of the jetty wall **Muro del Malecón (5),** was begun in 1901 from La Punta, to drain the sea front and make it look better. It took fifty years for it to arrive at the mouth of the river Almendares, seven kilometres distant. Constantly swept by the sea breeze and

The Gran Teatro seats 2,000 spectators.

Hotel Inglaterra, founded in 1856.

without great wooded areas on the urban perimeter, the city breathes through the lung provided by the jetty, toning down the rigours of the long summer. Since its creation it has been the Havanans' favourite place for relaxation, and the Mecca of their love affairs, when in the enchantment of the evenings and the friendly shelter of the night, the long wall becomes a long line of endless kisses...

Avenida Galiano (6) is reached by going left at the glass frontage of the Hotel Deuville. What is now a wide urban artery sprang from a small local path leading in the 18th century to the walled city. In 1860 it was already considered the capital city's most beautiful street and was its first large transversal street. The 20th century transformed it into one of the main shopping streets with large shops and stores. Galiano is like a clock measuring the city's pulse. Hurried pedestrians walk along it very early on their way to work, pushed for time. After ten in the morning and for the rest of the day it vibrates with shoppers exploring businesses and going through the open air displays. After five in the afternoon unhurried walkers amble till dusk. In this street, number 208, is an admirable building covered with mosaics from Seville which are a real joy to see. One block above, frozen in time which appears to have no effect on it, is the Church of Our Lady of Monserrate, the oldest construction in the avenue, dating from 1843. Next to the Church are the Galiano Art Gallery and opposite the Teatro América Cinema, interesting examples of Havana Art Deco.

Galiano and San Rafael constitute the epicentre of the avenue with the park and the entrance to the boulevard. From here to Zanja it has a uniform appearance flanked by turn of the century buildings and shops. We turn right at the junction with Zanja, in order to arrive at a colourful and always enigmatic place, the **Barrio Chino** **(7)** (Chinese Quarter).

The Cuchillo de Zanja district, a kind of little Beijing in the heart of Havana, is full of life both day and night. There is no other place in the city selling as many sweets as in, El Cuchillo nor can we find better tropical garden produce and fruit, grown by the ancestral painstaking skill of the descendants of Confucius.

The first Chinese arrived in Cuba 150 years ago. They were contracted to serve for eight years in exchange for a miserable wage which did not pay their return. Most of them stayed in Cuba, living with black women and mulattos, mixing blood and culture. In addition to the first Chinese a financially better-off group from California set up by the waters of the Zanja Real, attracted by advantages for investment and business. This original nucleus, by virtue of great persistence and hard work, put down the bases for the solid Asian community in Havana. It became the most prosperous in Latin America. Today the Barrio Chino has taken on new life due to their descendants' proposal to rescue its culture and traditions. Leaving the Barrio Chino the itinerary takes us along Calle Dragones towards Fraternity Park. Arrival here is easiest if we take as

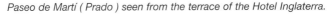

Paseo de Martí (Prado) seen from the terrace of the Hotel Inglaterra.

Buildings in Paseo del Prado.

reference the beautiful white tower belonging to the telephone company ETECSA, which stands out like those of a Florentine palace above the other buildings in the area.

In the 19th century, this was the Campo de Marte, where Spanish troops carried out ostentatious military exercises. It was also the place for great public festivities and events, such as the first ascents in a balloon in 1828. It had a chain pump which supplied part of the city with water for many years and a bull ring.

The **Fraternity Park (8)** (Parque de la Franternidad) in Havana is charmed in terms of views. Wherever we look it offers a different perspective, on one side the wide Avenida de la Reina which begins within it and may be seen along its entirety, and on the other the colossal sight of the Capitol, which fills the urban landscape in this area. In the centre the main colour is the green of the leafy giants of the native flora with its palm trees, yagrumas, majaguas and ceibas sown with earth from of all the American Republics, representing the tree of American brotherhood, after which the park was named in 1927. Diagonally opposite each other two 19th century gems close the perimeter, the Fountain of La India and the **Aldama Palace (9).**

The jetty, with Old Havana in the background.

El Cuchillo de Zanja.

Avenida Galiano.

The Palace constructed for a rich Basque, Don Domingo Aldama y Arrechaga, by the architect Manuel José Carrerá, was built in 1844 and is considered the maximum exponent of neoclassicism in Cuba. Of magnificent proportions, its simple but majestic façade contrasts with the line of columns raised on pedestals and crowned by Ionic capitals. Its interior has nothing to envy the most eminent European palaces, with its paintings of Pompeii, coloured marbles of various designs and carefully worked wrought-iron decorations. The furniture and works of art which decorated it were extremely luxurious. In 1868 all the fittings were sacked and destroyed by the Spanish Volunteer Corps, in revenge for the separatist leanings of Miguel Aldama, son of Domingo and the building's second owner. Restored a few years ago it is now the headquarters of the Cuban Institute of History.

The **Fountain of La India (10),** or of La Noble Habana as it is also known, is considered as one of the city's three symbols, with the El Morro Lighthouse and the Giraldilla in the Castle of La Real Fuerza. It was made in 1837 by the Italian sculptor Giusseppe Gaggini for the Count of Villanueva. It represents a lovely lady seated and adorned with feathers, on a wide pedestal surrounded by four dol-

Veteran automobiles in the Park of La Fraternidad.
Palace of Domingo Aldama.

Fountain of La India.

phins pouring water into the fountain from their mouths. For many years it was the beginning of the beautiful Alameda de Isabel II, which later became the Paseo del Prado.

Before continuing towards the Capitol, take the opportunity to plan a visit to the Partagás Tobacco Factory, founded in 1849 and one of the oldest working Havana cigar factories. It opens its doors to visitors from Monday to Friday from 10 in the morning for the first tour and 1.30 in the afternoon for the second.

It is in Calle Industria, on the corner with Dragones, at the bottom of the Capitol. It is very easy to identify due to its typical façade, with a hoarding above. For now, if it is not yet visiting time, you can always have a coffee there or a glass of mellow rum, completing this exultation of the senses with a good cigar chosen from among the varied offer of the best. There is a bar in the basement of the factory and a humidor for those who enjoy this ritual.

The **National Capitol (11)** is the high point of our tour. It would be sacrilege to try to describe this monumental in a few lines, so we shall make a brief sketch to leave to you the privilege of amazement and discovery.

Built to serve as the headquarters of the House of Representatives and the Senate, it was erected with hard Capellanía stone and the participation of more than two thousand workmen, craftsmen and master builders.

Park of American Fraternity.
Ceiba planted using soil from all the American republics.

The National Capitol.

A dozen famous Cuban architects and engineers also worked on this project. To date it has been the most complex and varied building architecturally in Cuba. The severe classical style predominates here, taken to admirable proportions.

The towns at the edge of Havana may be seen from its 94 metre cupola, as well some 40 miles out to sea. The grandiose staircase stands out in the main façade, with its two bronze statues 7 metres high and weighing 15 tons, and symbolising Work and the Guardian Virtue of the People, works by the Italian sculptor Angelo Zanelli, also author of the Altar of La Patria in Rome. The entrance portico is supported by very high magnificent columns. Exquisitely beautiful details are to be seen along its 200 metres of façade, such as the admirable frieze work by different authors. The interior of the Capitol is overwhelming. The monumental vestibule leads to the great central hall below the cupola, where there is a diamond and the statue to the Republic, also by Zanelli, one of the largest interior statues, 17.54 metres in height and weighing 49 tons. On both sides we observe the huge perspective of the Hall of the Lost Steps.

The library, the offices, conference halls and are of exclusive design, and not an imitation, as some have believed, of the Capitol in Washington.

The Capitol was inaugurated with great public festivities on 20 May 1929 and since 1960 has been the headquarters of the Academy of Sciences, currently the Ministry of Sciences, Technology and the Environment.

Salon of Los Pasos Perdidos in the National Capitol.

Simón Bolivar Room in the National Capitol.

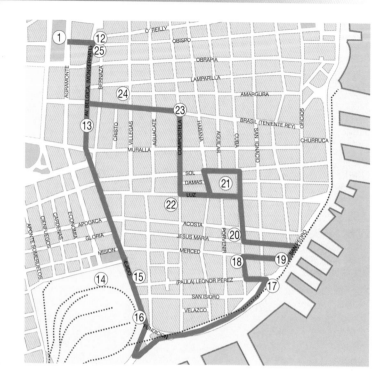

ITINERARY NUMBER TWO

12- Plazuela de Albear.
13- Calle Monserrate.
14- Central Railway Station
15- Birthplace of José Martí.
16- Puerta de la Tenaza (Tenail Gate).
17- Church of San Francisco de Paula.
18- Church of Nuestra Señora de la Merced.
19- Alameda de Paula.
20- Church of Spíritu Santo.
21- Convent and Church of Santa Clara of Asís.
22- Convent and Church of Belén.
23- Convent and Church of Santa Teresa.
24- Plaza del Cristo.
25- "El Floridita" Bar.

This second itinerary also leaves from the Central Park. We cross Calle Zulueta and go into Monserrate, passing between the impressive beautiful buildings of the Centro Asturiano and the Manzana de Gómez.

At this point we find the **Plazuela de Albear (12)** and the world famous restaurant "Floridita", a favourite haunt of writer Ernest Hemingway during the years he lived in Havana. Calle Obispo begins between them, going down towards the historical centre. This will later be the objective of one of the most interesting routes in this guide.

The Cuban engineer Don Francisco de Albear y Lara was immortalised in marble for resolving the greatest of Havana's problems since its founding, the water supply.

In the year 1856 Albear proposed a solution to the problem by building an aqueduct to take water from the fast-flowing Vento springs on the left bank of the river Almendares. The project was approved and finished in 1893. The conception of the work was sufficient to obtain a gold medal at the Paris Exhibition, and today it still brings water to the city which now has two million inhabitants. Albear died in 1897 and a few days later the town hall agreed to erect a statue to him. It was sculpted by the Cuban José Villalta de Saavedra, and inaugurated on 15 March 1895.

We shall leave the outline of the "Floridita" quite intentionally until the end of this route. We now continue to the right along **Calle Monserrate (13),** to Plaza de las Ursulinas, the beginning of Calle Egido, takes us to the Central Railway Station.

In Monserrate we are walking along the hollow once occupied by the walls of Old Havana, closing off the side facing the land. The street owes its name to a small chapel to the Virgin of Monserrate

Calle Monserrate.

Palace of the Countess of Villalba.

which existed between 1695 and 1836 at the junction with Calle O'Reilly, where a door with the same name also opened into the wall.

Along the street we see beautiful buildings constructed during the urbanisation process following the demolition of the walls. The ancient **Palace of the Countess of Villalba** stands out among them. Its colossal dimensions occupy 2300 m2 in front of Plaza de las Ursulinas. Its lavishness is compared with that of the Palace of Aldama and it was constructed in 1875 in a style inspired by the Italian renaissance.

Two blocks before the train terminal, in Egido between Gloria and Apodaca, there is another notable building, the **Palace of the Marquises of Balboa,** dated 1871. It was Havana's first private palace, occupying a whole block, surrounded by gardens and with a façade on all four sides. Unusually for the era, it did not follow the neoclassical canons imperative in the 19th century, but rather Madrid fashion which at the time was very influenced by small French palaces.

Opposite the Palace of Balboa is the "Puerto de Sagua" restaurant, specialising in fish and seafood dishes. The "Los Marinos" cafeteria is in the next block, next to the shopping centre of the same name. The **Central Railway Station (14)** is our next objective. Constructed on the ruins of the Arsenal, the most memorable of the Spanish shipyards, the station came into service in 1912. The old dream of uniting the island from Guane to Santiago de Cuba came true, with a railway more than one thousand kilometres long.

The Central Station building is a beautiful and functional exponent of public buildings, with its large waiting rooms and wide platforms. In the main hall is a valuable museum piece, the oldest locomotive in Cuba, "La Junta", dating from 1840. Cuba was the first country in Latin America to have a railway, inaugurated in 1837, before even Spain.

Leaving Central Station, along Calles Egido and Leonor Pérez, there is a discreet little park with trees. Next to this, painted yellow, is the **birthplace of José Martí y Pérez (15),** Cuban National Hero and Apostle of Independence, born on 28 January 1853.

The house, which was declared a museum in 1925, is often visited by children, for whom Martí had a special attachment. He left an exquisite book for them called "The Golden Age", a cultural framework of inestimable value.

Martí began his political life at 16 years of age, imprisoned on charges of treason. He was found with a letter upbraiding a fellow student for joining the Volunteer Corps. Condemned to forced labour in the San Lázaro quarries, he came out nearly one year later with his health broken for life. Deported to Spain he began a journey which would take him to Europe, Latin America and the United States, where he finally organised the struggle for liberation which he called the necessary war. He had to overcome innumerable set-

Central Railway Station.

31

The locomotive La Junta, built in 1840, the oldest in Cuba, on view at Central Station.

backs to achieve his objective, under the vigilance of Spanish spies who never lost track of him.

The insurrection finally broke out on 24 February 1895, and Martí returned to Cuba to join up as a soldier. Once he had said prophetically: "If I die, let it be facing the sun". On 19 May of that year he galloped off pistol in hand to meet a Spanish advance guard in the combat at Dos Ríos. The shots which caused his death made his body fall backwards with his forehead held high, so fulfilling his own prophecy.

José Martí, in addition to being the Hero of Independence, was a brilliant writer who took on nearly all prose and poetry subjects. The museum at his birthplace holds his complete works and a sample of his personal effects, manuscripts and testimonies on his family life. The street in front of the house is called Leonor Pérez in homage to the Apostle's mother.

After visiting Martí's house, continuing along Calle Egido, on the right pavement we see the largest stretch of wall still standing and the so-called **Puerta de la Tenaza (16).**

According to Emilio Roig Leuchsering, who acted for many years as the city's historian, the construction and demolition of the walls was "the greatest adventure" undertaken by Havana in colonial times.

The idea of walling the town was suggested as long ago as 1558, after the attack by the French pirate Jackes de Sores left it completely destroyed and utterly helpless. The lack of resources at that time meant the project was out of the question. Some streets facing the mountains were protected with weak adobe walls and wooden barricades.

The subject of the walls was taken up more seriously again in the 17th century, with the evaluation of a project presented by the engineer Cristóbal de Rodas, which also served to foreshadow the future town planning of Havana. The King arranged an annual budget of 20 thousand pesos from the Royal Chests in Mexico for this enterprise and even decreed an unusual tax to collect half a real for each half litre (approximately) of wine sold in the taverns.

The engineer Juan de Síscaras laid the first stone on 3 February 1674 and the city was completely surrounded, apart from a small opening for the mooring of ships, by 1740. 182 years had gone by since it had been thought of until its completion, and some 3 million pesos had been spent.

The walls were an average of 1.40 metres thick and 10 metres high, with a good masonry factory provided by the live rock on the coast.

Birth-place of Jose Martí.

Its perimeter was some 5 kilometres long. It was defended on the land side by nine bastions linked by stretches of wall protected by cannons. Each bastion had sentry boxes to shelter the guards. There were also covered paths with their parade grounds, moats and steep drops. The garrison comprised 3400 men, who could be doubled in an attack. There were 180 guns of different calibres. The wall opened its eleven doors in the morning at a shot from a single cannon and closed in the same way at night.

After imprisoning Havana for 123 years without any military glory, its demolition began on 8 August 1863 with an official ceremony. The task was not complete until the beginning of the 20th century . Of the old walls, apart from the few fragments left standing for old times' sake, we are left with the traditional cannon shot at nine in the evening. This is useful for putting watches right and for frightening the absorbed walkers on the Avenida del Puerto.

Leaving La Tenaza we continue to the left, entering the feverish activity of the port warehouses. You would never think now that this was the loneliest and saddest place in Havana 150 years ago. Those few people who ventured here called it Shelterless Street, the name it still has today. It only showed signs of life at the junction with the **Hospital and Church of San Francisco de Paula (17).**

The Church, mutilated and alone in the midst of the intense port traffic surrounding it, survived the demolition of its attached hospi-

Wall in Havana. La Tenaza.

Church of Santa Paula.

tal in 1946, thanks to a private company which purchased the land, an event which led to a loud protest from Havanans.

Fortunately the elements of great architectural value from the 18th century still remained in the church. Its octagonal dome is an important work in the religious city's baroque, as is its façade, where when the sun shines at an angle interesting shapes appear. The church of Paula is now under restoration and its archaeological legacy is being investigated.

From Paula we walk along Calle Leonor Pérez and turn right at the end of the block, into Calle Cuba, where we immediately see the **Church of Nuestra Señora de Merced (18).** It is sometimes compared with St. Peter's in Rome due to its disproportionate decoration. Its interior nave and the altar are unbelievably beautiful, and are unique among colonial churches.

La Merced was the aristocracy's favourite church for sumptuous weddings. Now, more modestly, but with just as much charm, young people continue to choose its altar for their ceremonies.

The monks of the San Vicente de Paúl Mission completed it in 1867, although it was begun in 1775. The faithful gather here in their thousands to worship on 24 September, feast day of the Virgin of the Merced, when they are allowed to go up to the great altar to pay tribute to their patron, decked in a rich white robe. The odd syncretisation of Catholic religious culture with African beliefs which took place in Cuba means that some worship Mary in the Virgen de La Merced, while others pay homage to Obatalá, Orisha, goddess of the earth and purity in the Yoruba religion.

On leaving the church we go down towards the sea along Calle Merced to the **Alameda de Paula (19)** with the O'Donnell Column in its centre. The pillar was sculpted in Italy and placed in the Alameda in 1847 by the Captain General of the Island, Leopoldo O'Donnell, in honour of the Spanish fleet and as part of the improvements made in the boulevard. The column is covered in relief work of military themes and crowned by a lion with the arms of Spain in its claws.

Paula Avenue or O'Donnell Hall as it was known after the erection of the pillar, was the first boulevard within the walls of Havana in the 18th century. Described in its era as one of the most pleasant places in the city, graced by its air and landscapes, it lost ground as other areas became fashionable. Today it still retains its ancient civic charm.

Front of the Church of Nuestra Señora de la Merced.

Nave in the Church of Nuestra Señora de la Merced.

Now we go back towards Cuba along Calle Jesús María, and after a short walk arrive at the **Church of Spíritu Santo (20),** the oldest in Havana after the old Parroquial Mayor Church.

Originally it was a chapel built by slaves and freed blacks in 1638. It was later extended and declared a parish church in 1674.

Outstanding in its interior are the baroque wooden lattice work gate and the large painting by the Cuban painter Arístides Fernández, both in the sacristy. In the baptistery we should mention the font by the sculptor Alfredo Lozano. It is considered a masterpiece of modern sculpture. The elaborate carpentry in the ceilings of the main nave is also worthy of mention.

During colonial times the Church of Spíritu Santo took on importance due to the Papal Bull of 1772 and the Royal Decree of 1773 of King Charles III, giving the right of asylum to those hunted by the authorities.

Other elements of interest are the funerary crypt and the sepulchre, together with the great altar with the recumbent statue of bishop Fray Gerónimo Valdés, again by Lozano.

Calle Cuba is noteworthy within Old Havana, not only because it bears the island's name, but also due to its historical buildings, cultural institutions and public buildings, lined along both sides of the street.

In Calle Cuba the Convent and **Church of Santa Clara of Asís (21)** are the next objective on our itinerary. It was founded in 1644 as the first nunnery in Havana, by a group of nuns from Cartagena de Indias.

The building is very large, occupying a huge rectangle consisting of four blocks between Habana, Cuba, Sol and Luz streets.

The beamed ceilings in its Church are worthy of note, as are the nuns' cells. The large patio of the Main Cloister, with abundant greenery and surrounded by wide galleries with arches and columns are an invitation to meditation and rest. There is a good angle for the belltower from here, which appears between the tree tops.

The Sailor's House, a typical Moorish house with wooden balconies, is located in the second cloister. Its name, according to legend, is due to its construction by a rich shipowner and pirate captain. He built it for his only daughter, who would not be persuaded out of her religious vocation.

The ancient convent of Santa Clara de Asís now hosts the National Centre of Conservation, Restoration and Museology, which played an active part in the work to recapture its old splendour.

O'Donnell's Column.

Church of Spíritu Santo.

Church of Nuestra Señora de Belén.

The Sailor's House **(Casa del Marino)** is home to the "Academic Residence", a moderately priced hostal for lovers of history and culture seeking a peaceful pleasant place in the heart of Old Havana.

Along Luz, the street where the Portuguese Antonio de la Luz y Do Cao opened the first post office in the 17th centuryand who gave it its name, we enter the Plaza del Convento de Belén.

The **Church and Convent of Belén (22),** dating from the 17th century, is located in Calle Compostela, from Calle Luz to Calle Acosta and meeting Calle Picota at the bottom. It was a refuge for poor convalescents under the auspices of Bishop Compostela. Belén is the first exponent of Havana's religious baroque, and the façade of its church is a fine example.

The Bethlehem monks, who had been exceptional in their charitable work for the poor, were ejected from the building in 1842. It was occupied by colonial government offices. It was made over to the Jesuits in 1854, who established a famous college for the sons of the aristocracy.

The archway over Calle Acosta, built to link the Convent with contiguous buildings, is the architectural element giving it personality, as well as the little square ahead in Calle Compostela, where there is a busy commercial spot selling farm products and Cuban tropical fruit.

Continuing on the right along the street taking the name of Bishop Compostela, famous for his virtues, we arrive at the **Church and Convent of Santa Teresa (23),** the last one built in Havana.

Worthy of the proverbial austerity of the Carmelite Order, it was built as a convent for the nuns. The most significant deed in its humble history was to receive the remains of Bishop Diego Evelino of Compostela, which rest in one of the most interesting sepulchres among the oldest in Cuba.

Its cloister was one of the largest and most attractive of the 18th century, with spacious airy rooms, ceilings with battens, wooden doors and windows with panels with mountings, grilles and balusters turned with exquisite wormanship. The church now yields cult to María the Helper.

Calle Teniente Rey, after Don Félix del Rey and Boza, who lived here and was the king's lieutenant on the Island, later renamed Brasil, brings us to **Plaza del Cristo (24).**

Named after the church located there, it was built in 1640 by agreement with the Town Council. Here the Franciscan fathers erected the Humilladero chapel, final goal of the Via Crucis procession on

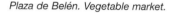

Plaza de Belén. Vegetable market.

Church and Convent of Santa Teresa, now consecrated to Maria Auxiliadora.

Main cloister in the Convent of Santa Clara de Asís.

Easter Fridays. They came up Calle de la Amargura from the Church of San Francisco de Asís.

From 1840 there was a market in the square with the picturesque name of "the washerwomen". Every day lively groups of old black women would gather in the square, most of whom washed clothes for a living. They went to mass at seven and then waited for the servants of the rich houses to ask for their services.

The square has undergone great changes, although around it there are still valuable examples of architecture from the 17th to the 19th centuries, such as Casa de la Parra converted today into the Restaurante Hanoi on the corner of Teniente Rey and Bernaza. The church still has its old façade, with two towers looking on to Calle Villegas. Its court once housed one of the oldest cementeries.

Admiring the imposing view of the Capitolio as we leave Teniente Rey for Monserrate, we turn to the right where a series of first class gastronomic centres open their doors to us and put us in the difficult position of having to choose.

The "Bar Monserrate" is first to receive us. It is typically Cuban in style, evoking the 40's. A step away is the "Castillo de Farnés", with a long tradition of Spanish cuisine and an excellent wine list.

Arch of Bethlehem in Calle Acosta.

"La Zaragozana", another of the greats in Spanish cuisine and seafood, is the foremost of all the restaurants in Havana. It retains the prestige gained over more than a century cultivating Iberian gastronomy.

Lastly, **"El Floridita" (25),** birthplace of the King of cocktails: the Daiquiri. There is no one better than Fernando G. Campoamor, distinguished investigator of rum and its culture, to tell the history of this famous bar-cum-restaurant, taking a fragment from his book, "The Happy Child of Sugar Cane":

The most famous Cuban bar, due to its great efficiency, is the "Floridita". Next to the Monserrate gate of the old wall and opposite Calle Obispo, "la Piña de Plata" operated here from 1820. When Constante (referring to Constantino Ribalaigua), the world famous barman, entered the business, it was known as "La Florida". This ended up as a fond diminutive, "El Floridita", listed among the first 10 bars in the world. Just as its Daiquiri is among the first 10 cocktails...

Hemingway converted the "Floridita" into his temple, recounting in his posthumous book, "Islands in the Gulf", how Constante weaved his frozen magic with lemon, sugar and rum.

Plaza del Cristo.
El Floridita.

ITINERARY III

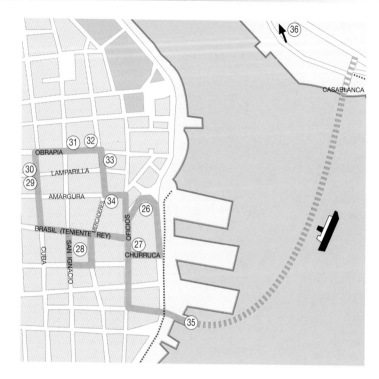

ITINERARY NUMBER THREE:

Our third itinerary begins in **Plaza de San Francisco (26).** This square is easily reached from any point in the city, just by taking a taxi or a short walk from the vicinity of the historic city centre.
The square was formed during the mid-16th century, long before the Franciscan convent and church were built. This was where fleets and armadas replenished their water supplies and loaded or unloaded goods. The square was a place of continuous bustling activity, with

a public market where transactions of all kinds took place. It was here also that emigrants from the Iberian Peninsula disembarked, carrying their dreams of quickly making their fortune in América.

From the beginnings of the 17th century, Capitans General and distinguished residents of Havana all had their homes in the vicinity of Plaza de San Francisco. Nearby was the seat of the Chapter, the prison and the customs house. Each October, the square was the venue for the great *Fiestas de San Francisco,* a festivity into which the local people threw themselves whole-heartedly.

The **Church and Convent of San Francisco de Asís (27),** which adjoins one of the sides of the square, giving the plaza its name, was completed in 1738 on the site of an earlier church built in the 16th century, but which was destroyed by a storm.

For many years, San Francisco was the most fashionable and elegant church in Havana. The nobles of the city were buried here throughout the 17th and 18th centuries, governors, generals, admirals, lords of Castile and even a vicereine of Peru.

It is also claimed that Saint Francis Solano, canonised by the Catholic Church for his labours of love, once lived in the convent. The most outstanding feature of this church, whose interior is composed of a nave and two aisles, is its belltower, which stands over the main entrance and was the highest in the city during colonial times. The front still conserves, worn by time, sculptures of the Immaculate Conception, Saint Francis of Assisi and Saint Domingo Guzmán.

Night-time view of Plaza de San Francisco.

Church of San Francisco de Asís. Calle de los Oficios.

Though simple, the convent was vast and beautiful, with three spacious cloisters, various courtyards and 111 cells for members of the religious community. In 1841, when the Spanish government confiscated the goods of the Church, the church and convent ceased to celebrate religious services and were converted into warehouses. During the 20th century the buildings were used as the headquarters of various official bodies until the site was finally restored in the early-1990s. The church, which has excellent acoustics, is now used as a museum and concert hall.

Plaza de San Francisco as we see it today is irregular in form, made up of the church, the goods exchange and Calles Oficios and San Pedro, which lead to the Avenida del Puerto.

The **Goods Exchange** -Lonja del Comercio- one of the most interesting buildings in the square, was built in 1909 as the Chamber of Representatives. It is the work of the architects Zoraya and Muir, in a somewhat ornamental neoclassical style. It has five storeys crowned by a dome at the top of which is a reproduction of the god Mercury in bronze by Juan de Bolonia.

Calle Oficios, one of the oldest streets in Havana, urbanised in the first half of the 16th century, contains several houses of a markedly Mudéjar style, as can be seen by their wooden balconies, the arrangement of the rooms and the inner courtyards and ornamental motifs. The street now contains many art galleries and the studios of renowned artists: the central courtyard of the house of Venezuelan painter Carmen Montilla Tinoco, at Calle Oficios 162, is adorned by an enormous ceramic mural by the sculptor Alfredo Sosabravo. Next, at number 166, is the studio and art gallery of Nelson Domínguez.

Leaving Calle de los Oficios and taking Calle Teniente Rey, we reach **Plaza Vieja (28).** This was known at the time of its construction in 1559 as Plaza Nueva. It was opened up as a public space after the original Plaza de la Iglesia (now Plaza de Armas) was given over to the royal troops for military exercises.

The square gradually took urban shape between the 17th and 18th centuries with the construction of a series of highly uniform houses both as regards their architecture and domestic arrangement. These occupied the perimeter of Calles San Ignacio, Mercaderes, Teniente Rey and Muralla. These were noble mansions of a peculiar style which was soon to become fashionable in the rest of the city, characterised by their porticoes supported by column, ideal for the tropical sun and rain, wooden balconies and tiled roofs.

These fine palaces include particularly the **House of El Conde de San Juan de Jaruco,** at Calle Muralla numbers 107 and 111, on the corner with Calle San Ignacio. Its architecture is typical of Plaza Vieja, with the singular element of the coloured glasses which adorn

Nave of the Church of San Francisco.

Exchange building.

the front of the second floor. These are amongst the most complex in the whole of Havana. The spacious salons of this mansion was graced by the cream of Havanan society and by the most illustrious foreigners. It was also the birthplace of María Mercedes de Santa Cruz y Cárdenas, the famous Countess of Merlín, who dazzled 19th-century Havana with the grace and style of her literary works. Calle San Ignacio number 364, the **House of El Conde de Casa Lombillo,** enjoys a magnificent position in the centre of the square. This mansion has a loggia with balcony and a portal of three arches. Its front is made up of a portal with pediment and columns over high pedestals. The building is adorned by valuable mural paintings dating to the 18th century which are presently being recovered and restored. On this same side of the street, at the end of the block at San Ignacio number 352 on the corner with Teniente Rey, is another notable dwelling, the **House of Las Hermanas Cárdenas.** This belonged to two women renowned for their piety, Doña María Loreto and Doña María Ignacia Cárdenas. Like the houses previously described, this building is developed around a central patio overlooked by the upper and lower galleries. Some of its most outstanding features are the mixtilíneo arch which dominates the entrance to the hall and its baroque carpentry, representative of that of the 18th century. For some time from the first third of the 19th century onwards, the Philharmonic Society, of enormous social and artistic importance, had its seat here. It is now occupied by the Ministry of Culture's Visual Arts Development Centre.

On the opposite side of the road, at Mercaderes number 307, is the **House of Beatriz Pérez Borroto,** which now houses the Cuban Photographic Library. Built in the 18th century, this was not one of the most oppulent palaces in the area, though it has a pretty front with portal with three arches and a loggia opening in an arch supported by pilasters on the second floor commanding panoramic views of the square.

Finally, at number 315, on the corner of Mercaderes and Muralla, is the **House of Franchi Alfaro,** whose architecture is unusual for the rest of the square as its portal is adorned with baroque decoration. Another very unusual element is found on the corner of San Ignacio and Muralla. This is the **oldest traffic sign in Havana,** dating back to the times when Calle Muralla was called Calle de Ricla in memory of the Count of the same name who came to Cuba in 1763, as Governor and Capitan General, to restore the power of Spain over the island at the end of the English occupation.

Amongst other adornments, the plaque reads: "Calle de Ricla, in memory of his Excellency the Count of Ricla, sent by His Majesty to restore this city. Year 1763".

Dusk over the Bay of Havana.

Plaza Vieja.

We now continue our visit by taking Calle Teniente Rey (Brasil), turning right into Calle Cuba. At the end of the first block are two outstanding buildings: the **Carlos J. Finlay Historic Museum of the Sciences (29),** and the former **Convent and Church of San Agustín,** now of San Francisco de Asís.

The building which now houses the museum was, from 1868, the headquarters of the Royal Academy of Medical, Physical and Natural Sciences of Havana, as well as the first Cuban museum of its kind, eventually succeeded by the present museum, which contains valuable collections relating to the history of the medical sciences in Cuba and important documents dating to the 19th century on the research which led the Cuban sage Carlos J. Finlay to the discovery of the Aedes Aegipti mosquito as the transmitter of yellow fever. The building also has a library with 95,000 books and an extraordinary historic painting collection. The building which houses it is also a veritable jewel of 19th-century architecture. In its hemicycle, scientist Albert Einstein gave his last public address during a visit to Havana in 1930.

Adjoining the Science Museum is the **Church of San Agustín (30),** consecrated in 1842 to Saint Francis of Assisi after the bishopric of Havana gave it to the community of Franciscans as compensation for the loss of the church of the same name as the square. The original building dates to 1633, when it was devoted to the hermits of Saint Augustine. Nevertheless, the building we now see was rebuilt and much altered in 1925.

The church has an architectural feature most uncommon in Cuban colonial architecture: the marked influence of rich Mexican art, behind which is the hand of the Augustine monks who designed it and who reached Cuba from Mexico. This singular feature is observed in the undulating pinion of the front, composed of tiny curves and countercurves, the only example of the use of such forms in the gable ends of our 17th-century churches.

The church has a broad nave with six altars and an artistic mural by the painter Martínez Andrés. The organ is one of the finest in the entire country.

Taking Calle Cuba in the same direction, we reach Obrapía where, on the corner of the two streets is the **House of Gaspar Riveros de Vasconcelos (31),** easily-recognised due to the corner balcony on the second floor.

This is esteemed to be the oldest house conserved in Havana, constructed as it was in the first half of the 17th century. Its most outstanding feature is the above-mentioned running balcony, which gives that section of the house the character of a lookout tower. The woodwork of the delicately curved balustrades, of the banisters and doors, give the work special value as an example of the early period when the characteristic elements of the Cuban house were beginning to take shape. The building was completely restored in 1985.

We now continue along Obrapía towards Mercaderes, where we find two interesting porticoes. The first stands at **number 60,** and was for-

House of Beatriz Pérez Borroto, now the Cuban Photographic Library.

French pharmacy, Carlos J. Finlay Science Museum.

merly that of Jacome Justiniani, a descendant of an Italian family which settled in Havana in the 16th century. Strangely, the entrance to this simple house is adorned with a fine, ingeniously-conceived portal. Composed of two side columns, it supports a curving pediment broken by a rose window and two decorative spirals in the centre.

Almost at the end of the street, on the same side, is another splendid portal. The design of this house is original and unique, conceived and built in Cadiz in around 1686. This is the **House of La Obrapía (32),** from which the street takes its name. The denomination is due to the installation of an *Obra Pía* (house of charity) here by Martin Calvo de la Puerta, owner of the building, to give economic support to five young orphans each year and allow them to form a family a.

The house stands out amongst those of its period. It is 1,480 m2 in size, making it also one of the largest of its time. Its courtyard, surrounded by columns, features a variety of semicircular, trefoiled and splayed arches. The House of La Obrapía is now a colonial museum, as well as housing a permanent exhibition on the life and works of the famous Cuban writer Alejo Carpentier.

Exactly opposite the House of Obrapía, in another old colonial palace is the **House of Africa,** a museum which houses President Fidel Castro's magnificent African Collection, with items from 26 countries, and the Afro-Cuban Collection of the prestigious researcher and ethnologist, Don Fernando Ortíz. At this centre, research goes on into the cultural and ethnic questions illustrated in the collections, particularly those with the most important influence on Cuban culture.

Reaching the intersection of Calles Obrapía and Mercaderes, we come to **Plaza de Simón Bolivar (33).** The area around this little square is of great interest as the epicentre of important museums housed in buildings of extraordinary historical and architectural value. On the left-hand side of the square is the **House of Benito Juárez,** devoted to the exhibition and dissemination of subjects relating to Mexican history, art and culture. In Calle Obrapía, after the building dedicated to Mexican culture is the **house of the painter Osvaldo Guayasamín,** with his studio and art gallery with a permanent exhibition of the works of Guayasamín and temporary exhibitions of Cuban and Latin American.

Opposite, in the little square leading into Mercaderes, is the **Simón Bolivar House,** devoted to the memory of the Liberator of the Americas, with a collection of artworks illustrating the great man's achievements. This house also serves as the venue for travelling exhibitions. In the 19th century, the building belonged to Santiago C. Burnham, and features finely-worked iron railings and a marble staircase as well as fine chrome crystal arches in the galleries of the upper floor. The central patio, home to birds and plants, is especially charming.

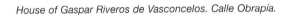

House of Gaspar Riveros de Vasconcelos. Calle Obrapía.

House of the Counts of Jaruco.

Continuing along Mercaderes, opposite the Simón Bolivar House, is the **Museo de La Armería** (Military Museum), the one of the principal scenes of the actions of the clandestine armed struggle in the 1950s. During the strike of 9 April 1958, the *armería* -armoury- was attacked by a revolutionary commando which carried off arms to send to the guerrilla, led by Fidel Castro, in the Sierra Maestra.

Mercaderes, a busy trading street since the 16th century and laid out at the same time as Calle de Oficios, making these the two oldest streets in Havana, leads to Calle Lamparilla, where a small exhibition room renders homage to the firefighters of Havana and commemorates the catastrophe of the Isasi Ironmonger's, which formerly stood on this site and was the cause of great mourning in the city in 1890. On 17 May 1890, a devastating fire broke out, causing a tremendous explosion in the building, which collapsed on top of the firemen and bystanders nearby. It was later found out that the owner of the premises had broken the ban on keeping explosive substances within the bounds of the city, and that he had not informed the fire brigade of this when they came to put out the fire. The accident cost the lives of 28 members of the fire brigade, including their chiefs. The funeral for these brave firefighters were the most important celebrated in Havana in the 19th century.

A block further on, at the corner of Amargura and Mercaderes, is an unusual green cross with two arms, opposite which is a house of striking architectural design. This house, number 231, is now the House of Students and was built in 1728, when it belonged to Francisco A. de Basabe. The balcony running across the front is a highly distinctive feature of the house, which is built around a spacious central courtyard. The Green Cross, or **Cruz Verde (34),** was the first of the stations of the procession which started out from the Church of San Francisco at Lent in the 18th and 19th centuries. Many cities and towns in Cuba, Mexico and Spain have streets with the name of La Amargura ("Bitterness") after the Stations of the Cross in Jerusalem, which was also thus known. Each Lent evening, a Passion emerged from the Third Order of Saint Francis, parading around the streets and stopping at the stations at the street corners, adorned by the local people with altars and crosses.

Calle Amargura leads us back to Calle Oficios, where we pass by the front of the Church of San Francisco and continue to the Plazuela del **Muelle de Luz (35).**

Painstaking restoration of the whole of Calle de Oficios has permitted the recuperation of a large number of colonial houses of great historic and architectural interest. In Plazuela de Luz is the **House of the Count of Casa Barreto,** at Calle Oficios number 362 on the corner with Calle de la Luz. This typical 18th-century building now houses the Provincial Centre for Plastic Art and Design.

To reach the last point on this itinerary, the statue of **El Cristo de La Habana (36),** we have to take a launch at the jetty known as the Muelle de Luz. Here, a short, pleasant boat trip will see us in the township of Casablanca on the other side of the bay.

Casablanca is a charming, peaceful seafaring village whose principal activity is centred in the shipyards and the Hersey train, the only electric train in Cuba for over 80 years and which still makes

Monumental doorway to the House of La Obrapía.

The statue of El Cristo de Havana.

the daily journey between Havana and the city of Matanzas more than one hundred kilometres to the east.

In order to reach the statue of Christ we have to go up the street opposite the jetty in Casablanca, crossing over at the amphitheatre and going between two houses to find the steps leading up to the Meteorological Institute and from here turning left to find the statue itself. It is also possible to reach this site along the road which runs past the amphitheatre, also turning left. Nevertheless, we consider the path up the steps to be much more interesting and enjoyable. Once at the top, the prize for our efforts will be the chance to enjoy a splendid view of Havana from a colossal height. El Cristo de La Habana is a monumental statue in white Carrara marble with a height of 15 metres. It stands on a three-metre-high pedestal which, taking into account the altitude of the hill on which it, in turn, stands, gives it a total height of 79 metres above sea level. The figure of Christ stands looking towards the city, one hand on His chest and the other raised in the act of blessing.

The statue is the work of the Cuban sculptor Jilma Madera, who carried out the work in Italy. The Christ of Havana is considered the largest sculpture in the world by a woman. It stands on an esplanade stretching from the Fortress of La Cabaña to the Meteorological Institute. It was inaugurated on 25 December 1958.

House of Simón Bolívar, upper floor.

The "Green Cross".
Plaza de Simón Bolívar.

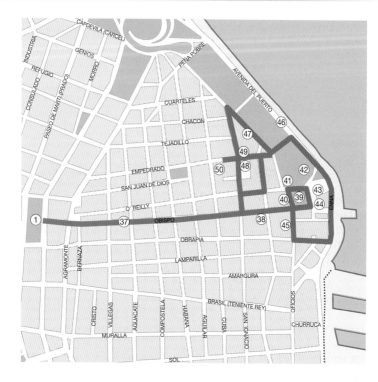

ITINERARY NUMBER FOUR:

37- Bulevar de Obispo.
38- Hotel "Ambos Mundos".
39- Plaza de Armas.
40- Palace of the Captains General.
41- Palace of El Segundo Cabo.
42- Castle of La Real Fuerza.
43- El Templete.
44- House of the Counts of Santovenia (Hotel Santa Isabel)
45- House of Los Arabes.
46- Avenida del Puerto.
47- Council Seminary of San Carlos and San Ambrosio.
48- Plaza de la Cathedral.
49- Havana Cathedral.
50- Bodeguita del Medio.

From Central Park, we enter the Plazuela de Albear, which we have already visited, at the top of Calle Obispo, leading us towards the historic city centre.

Bulevar de Obispo (37) has been one of the busiest and most cosmopolitan of all the streets of Havana for over 200 years. Its name ("Bishop Boulevard") is attributed to the predilection felt for it by Bishop Pedro Agustín Morell of Santa Cruz in the 18th century. From its very beginnings it has been a busy shop-lined street which flourished particularly in the 19th century when it was the main thoroughfare connecting the walled city with the quarters outside the walls through the Monserrate Gate. It was through this gate that a large part of fruits of the field entered Havana.

Just as in olden days, Calle Obispo is lined on either side with shops and businesses as well as bars and cafés whose decor is very much in the *retro* style. These include "La Lluvia de Oro" in Obispo y Habana and the beloved "Café París" on the corner with San Ignacio two blocks before we come to the Plaza de Armas.

In the early-1930s, when the writer Ernest Hemingway began living in Havana, he would often be seen strolling along Calle Obispo at any time of the night or day, heading for the "Floridita" or back to the Hotel "Ambos Mundos" after imbibing a few of his large iced daiquiris.

Very narrow due to having been laid out in accordance with the colonial norm, which limited the width of streets in places with a warm climate, Calle Obispo has no porticoes, but it does have relatively high buildings, some of the truly imposing, which protect it from the street throughout practically the whole day. The most outstanding of these buildings, which for the most part date back to the early-20th century, is that which during the 1920s housed the

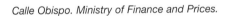

Calle Obispo. Ministry of Finance and Prices.

National Bank of Cuba and now belongs to the Ministry of Finance and prices. This building stands on the corner of Obispo and Cuba. Like other similar edifices distributed in an area of around two square kilometres, this palace once formed part of the so-called Banking District, a kind of small Wall Street in the heart of Havana where a group of foreign banking institutions had their business centres. All of these buildings shared a similar luxurious decor and monumental and academic style of architecture.

In what were formerly the Vaults of the old National Bank is now a curious **Finance Museum** exhibiting, in an excellent state of conservation, the enormous safe which held the nation's reserves for over half a century.

Leaving behind us Calle San Ignacio, not without calling a brief halt in the Café París to refresh ourselves with a fine local beer taken very cold as is the Cuban custom, we now head towards the **Hotel "Ambos Mundos" (38)** at the end of the block.

This hotel is a place of cult in Havana, and was Hemingway's base during his journeys to Cuba after 1932. Once there, he invariably took room 511 on the fifth floor, from where he could observe the environs of Plaza de la Catedral, part of the port and some of the oldest roofs in the city which more than once inspired his work. It was here that Hemingway wrote some of his finest journalistic pieces, particularly those describing fishing in the Gulf Stream, his

Hotel Ambos Mundos.

Funeral stone of Doña Maria de Cepero, the oldest in Cuba (1557).

Colonial houses in Calle Obispo.

"Great Blue River". It was also in this hotel that he began the final draft of "For Whom the Bell Tolls".

Opposite the "Ambos Mundos", taking Obispo, where we now see the modern Ministry of Education building, formerly stood the first University of Cuba, founded in 1728. This university had the name of **Royal and Pontifical University of San Jerónimo de La Habana** and was housed in the Convent of Santo Domingo. In 1842, it became a lay institution, separate from the convent, and it was demolished just a few years later, and all that remains of it is its old bell, which hangs between two high columns.

As we continue down the street we find, on our left, the Palace of Los Capitanes Generales and, now uncovered, part of the tunnels which gave access to its underground crypt. On the right is an interesting series of houses dating back to the 17th century. Number 121-123 is a mansion distinguished by its beautiful running balcony on the corner of Obispo and Mercaderes; next is the splendid palace of Antonio Hoces Carrillo, with a delightful inner courtyard, spacious apartments and delicate carpentry. This house is marked by the numbers 117-119. At Obispo number 113 is the palace known as La Casa de la Orfebrería, exhibiting an outstanding collection of luxurious silver articles dating to the colonial period.

On the same side of the road, in the building which was, in 1688, the **San Francisco de Sales College** for orphan girls, its architecture little changed from the original, is the restaurant establishment "La Mina", which specialises in Cuban cuisine and shellfish. Cafeteria and snack bar services, open 24 hours a day, are also available at the "Al Capuccino Habana", Bar "La Terraza" and La Cremería, which serves exquisite Coppelia ice creams made from tropical fruit. The upper floors of "La Mina" are occupied by the studios and workshops of renowned Cuban plastic artists.

We now come out into **Plaza de Armas (39),** its colonial beauty set off by leafy trees, well-tended flower gardens and the cheerful fleeting chirping of sparrows splashing in the little fountains of the park. The city's largest old and used book market takes place here every day of the week except Mondays, offering rare books, curios and discontinued editions.

In the 16th century, the centre of the old city was a little square around which the inhabitants erected their modest dwellings. This square was on the site of what is now the Castle of La Real Fuerza. When it was decided to build the castle here, a nearby site was also chosen for a new square, known in those days as Plaza de la Iglesia, as the town's only church stood here.

In 1581, the serious conflict between the governor of the castle, Diego Quiñones, and the Cuban Governor, Gabriel Luján, over the control of the 200 soldiers who then made up the castle garrison, Quiñones demonstrated his supremacy by taking over the square for the purpose of carrying out military exercises. Despite the

Plaza de Armas (parade ground).

La Giraldilla, symbol of the city.

Fountain of Neptune.

protests of the population, nothing could be done to prevent this, and even the name of the square was eventually changed to Plaza de Armas - Parade Ground.

With the passing of time, new fortresses were built, provided with large military zones which enabled the square to be freed from its bellicose occupants and the local residents to enjoy the spot once more. The demolition of the Parroquial Mayor Church in the 18th century, as it had been badly damaged by shrapnel and rigging from His Majesty's Ship "Invencible", which blew up in 1741 after being struck by lightning, brought with it the extension, rehabilitation and improvement of the hitherto rather unattractive square. Later, during the periods in office of governors Apodaca and Dionisio Vives, it was installed with fountains, trees and flowerbeds. Historians, scholars and visitors alike agree that the Plaza de Armas was of extraordinary importance as a place of leisure in colonial times. For many years, nighttime retreats were celebrated here, watched from his palace balcony by the Captain General whilst the aristocratic ladies of Havana rode in their carriages through the surrounding streets and the gentleman strolled in the park or sat on the benches or hired chairs.

Having been restored on various occasions, the Plaza de Armas now has the aspect it had in 1841, rebuilt according to engravings of the period, only the statue changed, that of King Ferdinand VII replaced by that of the Father of the Patria, Carlos Manuel de Céspedes, who declared the First War of Independence on 10 October 1868.

Palace of the Captains General. City Museum.

Taking a clockwise stroll around the square, the first monument we see is the **Palace of the Captains General (40),** which began to be built in 1776 on the site of the former Parroquial Mayor Church. The palace was designed by Havanan architect Antonio Fernández Trevejos with the participation of Pedro Medina. Both were under the direct supervision of the Captain General Felipe Fonsdeviela, Marquis of La Torre, a renowned Spanish governor and town planner. The palace was inaugurated by the Illustrious Don Luis de las Casas in 1791, after which it served as the seat of the Spanish government for over a century until 1898, when Spain lost sovereignty over the island. From 1899 to 1902, it was the residence of the North American government of intervention and was later the seat of the republican government until 1920. Moreover, the sessions of the Havana Mayor's office took place in its salons for 176 years until 1967, when restoration work began on it before it was opened one year later as the City of Havana Museum. The Palace of the Captains General is the most important of all those inherited from the colonial period. Along with the Palace of El Segundo Cabo and the cathedral, it forms a trilogy of what is known as "Cuban baroque", with more austere lines and neoclassical influence. The City Museum housed in the palace features diverse exhibits illustrating the history of Havana. Of particular interest are the archaeological collection and those of sculptures and carriages, as well as the sumptuous 18th- and 19th-century furniture and the rooms dedicated to the wars of independence from 1868 until 1959.

In the palace courtyard is a fine sculpture of Christopher Columbus, standing and in period dress. This statue was made in Italy by the sculptor Garbeille, and dates to 1862. Under the right-hand gallery, almost in the centre, embedded in the wall is the oldest monument in Cuba, erected to the memory of Doña María de Cepero in the year 1557, when she died, victim of a blunderbuss shot whilst attending a religious ceremony in the **Parroquial Mayor.** In this same gallery, on the right, at the foot of the stairs leading to the mezzanine rooms, is the original sculpture of the Giraldilla, the first made in bronze, dating to 1634, and the work of Havanan founder and sculptor Gerónimo Martínez Pinzón. A replica of this work adorns the keep of the Castle of La Real Fuerza, where the original was first installed.

Opposite the main entrance to the Palace of the Captains General is the only stretch of road with wooden paving stones which exists in the entire country.

In Calle O'Reilly, closing one side of the square, is the **Palace of El Segundo Cabo (41).** This palace was planned by the Marquis of La Torre and was originally intended to house the Royal Post Office. It was completed in 1772, also under the direction of Trevejos. Its imposing portal with broad doorway, supported by robust columns and which was the model for that of the Palace of the Captains General, gives access to a square patio surrounded by arches forming a combination with clear Andalusian influences. It served only for a very short time as the Post Office, passing almost imme-

Palace of El Segundo Cabo.

diately into the possession of the Tax Inspectorate which occupied the building exclusively. In 1853, Sub-Inspector Segundo Cabo was authorised to install his offices there. During the 20th century, it was the Palace of the Senate, Supreme Court of Justice, National Academy of Arts and Letters, seat of the Cuban Geographical Society and is now the headquarters of the Cuban Book Institute.

The next objective of our tour of the Plaza de Armas is the **Castle of La Real Fuerza (42).** This had its antecedents in a fortress built in 1540 by Captain Mateo Aceituno at the orders of Governor Hernando Soto, shortly before he began his journey to Florida from which there was to be no return. In his absence, he named his wife, Doña Isabel de Bobadilla as governess in his place. Doña Isabel is the only woman in the history of Cuba to have held this high office. According to legend, Doña Isabel scanned the horizon day after day as she waited for her husband to return. De Soto, however, the discover of the Mississippi, died victim of fever. It is said that this legend inspired Gerónimo Martín Pinzón to produce the image of the Giraldilla.

The old castle was destroyed in 1555 by the pirate Jackes de Sores, after which the present Castle of La Real Fuerza, much stronger than the earlier stronghold, was built. With an excellent stonemason's shop, which has been preserved in a good   state of repair, building began in 1558 under the direction of the engineer Bartolomé Sánchez and was completed 20 years later in 1577 by the High Master of Works Francisco Calona.

Castle of La Real Fuerza.

Castle of La Real Fuerza, seen from La Cabaña.

Strongly garrisoned and equipped for defence, the castle was nevertheless very badly situated strategically, far from the entrance to the bay and surrounded by buildings which would have caused a serious obstacle to its guns in any attack. However, it played a merely dissuasive role throughout its history, as it did not even have time to enter into combat during the conquest of Havana by the English in 1762, as the city surrendered once El Morro had fallen, long before the enemy had entered the range of its cannons. In times of peace the castle was used to house various official institutions, the most noble of them the National Library. It is now a gallery with a permanent exhibition of Cuban ceramics. The roof terraces offer restaurant and cafeteria services.

Less than 20 metres from the castle is a tiny replica of the Parthenon in Athens, constituting one of the most interesting monuments in the whole of Havana: **El Templete (43),** or small temple. This was the first neoclassical building in the city and is traditionally associated with the celebration of the First Mass and the First Chapter on 19 November 1519, under a leafy ceiba tree which is said to have stood near here. It was inaugurated in 1828 with great festivity at the behest of the Captain General, Don Francisco Dionisio Vives, and with the wholehearted support of Bishop Espada.

In the interior of the Templete are three large paintings by the French artist Juan Bautista Vermay. The work on the left recreates the ceremony of the First Chapter and the one on the right the First

Mass, whilst the painting in the centre reproduces the official inauguration of the monument with all the personalities which attended the even. The remains of Vermay and his wife are conserved in a marble urn.

Outside is a commemorative pillar predating the construction of the Templete, dating to the year 1754. This was erected by the then Governor, Don Francisco Cajigal. The tiny bust is a rare representation of Christopher Columbus with a moustache. The ceiba is the only surviving specimen of the three planted in 1828. According to an age-old tradition, each 19 December, anniversary of the founding of Havana, the people of the city go round the ceiba three times to ask it for three wishes.

Behind the Templete is Calle Enna, the smallest street in Havana, beginning and ending on either side of the monument.

We next come to the lordly former **House of the Counts of Santovenia (44).** This, after large-scale alteration and restoration, has recovered the function it began to fulfil in 1867 as the Hotel Santa Isabel, favoured by lovers, traders, artists and illustrious travellers in the 19th century. The Santa Isabel, which enjoys a highly privileged location in the heart of Old Havana, has three floors occupying practically the entire block. Its present arrangement dates to 1784, respected during its recent restoration. With its palatial air, the hotel is now an elegant five-star establishment with 27 rooms, 10 of them suites, offering all the services compatible with its luxury status.

Suite in the Hotel Santa Isabel.

Front of the Hotel Santa Isabel.

Closing the circle around the square we return once more to Calle Obispo, turning left at the corner with La Mina to take Calle de los Oficios, with the air of an authentic colonial street which has imbued it since it was the first street in the city to be laid out far back in the 16th century.

At Oficios number 8, past the butcher's, on the right-hand side, is the **Numismatic Museum.** This possesses the largest collection of Cuban coins from all times, including 20 gold coins of enormous value. The building dates to the 17th century and was for many years the residence of the bishops of Havana, serving as the Bishop's Palace until 1858. After 1844 it also housed the Monte de Piedad or pawnbroker's. The next house on the same side of the street formed part of the former **College of San Ambrosio** from 1689 until 1774. It is of simple architecture with pleasant interior environment, but it not only delights the aesthetic taste, but also tempts the palate, housing in its upper floors the Al Medina restaurant, which specialises in Arabic cuisine.

Opposite, our attraction is drawn to the veteran cars of the **Automobile Museum.** The first car was driven around Havana, causing stupor and surprise, in December 1898. The museum contains a splendid collection of epoch-making vehicles, many of which still circulate around the streets and roads of Cuba.

At Calle Oficios number 16 is the **House of Los Arabes (45),** containing collections of Oriental art, costume and other objects recreating the age-old culture of the eastern civilisations. From the times of the conquest, Cuba received Arab emigrants who left a deep mark on the national culture. The House of Los Arabes devotes part of its institutional activity to the study and recuperation of the Morisco spirit.

At the junction with Calle Obrapía, before moving on towards Avenida del Puerto, we can visit the charming **Hostal Valencia,** installed in a noble old house built in the 17th century, at Oficios number 53. This was the residence of Governor Count Sotolongo, an illustrious member of the Spanish nobility with an outstanding pedigree. The Hostal has twelve rooms and highly personalised service. It also boasts the best restaurant specialising in paellas in the entire city.

Calle Obrapía leads us to the open space of the bay along broad **Avenida del Puerto (46),** also Avenida Carlos Manuel Céspedes. This street forms a prolongation of the jetty towards the canal of the bay. It begins in La Punta and ends at the Terminal de Cruceros opposite Plaza de San Francisco. Its construction entailed reclaiming, filling in and drying over one hundred metres from the canal providing entrance to the bay. A stroll along Avenida del Puerto should be taken slowly to allow us to fully enjoy the delights and beauties of this truly splendid landscape. Casa Blanca, the El Cristo statue, La Cabaña, the Port,

Havana Cathedral. Nave.

Front of Havana Cathedral.

the township of Regla, El Morro, everything appears in a panoramic view as we feel the sea breeze, full of that peculiar smell of the sea and the port, a mixture of pitch and saltpetre...

Where Plaza de Armas opens to lead into Avenida, there is an obelisk commemorating one of the events of the Second World War: the sinking by German submarines of five Cuban merchant ships and the death of 77 seamen, whose names are engraved in a bronze plaque on the monument.

Cuba formally declared war on the Axis countries towards the end of 1941. In 1942, in an operation which would have made a fantastic film, the arrest was made of the German spy who sent information about the arrival and departure of merchant ships from Havana. These ships were subsequently hunted on the high seas by submarines. Heinz August Kunning, under the assumed name of Enrique Augusto Lunin, worked for the Nazi intelligence services, for which he was tried and condemned to death. He was executed on 10 November 1942.

Our itinerary along Avenida del Puerto now takes us to the beautiful **Fountain of Neptune** (Fuente de Neptuno), carved in Carrara and installed in 1838, originally at the intersection of Prado and Calle Neptuno, near Central Park.

We now take Calle Empedrado, we runs between Explanada la Fuerza and the Parque de la Avenida del Puerto, turning right into Calle Tacón, until we reach the building of the former **Council Seminary of San Carlos y San Ambrosio (47),** now Archbishopric of Havana, founded in 1724 by the Company of Jesus.

The front facing Tacón is not the original, but dates to the 1950s, when the building underwent alteration. The style of the building is neobaroque and takes its inspiration from the front of Havana Cathedral.

At the foot of the seminary is an excavation site showing the foundations of what formerly formed part of the sea front section of the city walls, corresponding to the so-called **Cortina de Valdés.** Before work began on Avenida del Puerto, the sea reached to with-

Automobile Museum.

Upper floor of the Palace of the Marquises of Aguas Claras.

in little more than ten metres from the wall of the Seminary of San Carlos. The cannons emplaced in this area are of little military significance, having been installed her to simulate a battery during the war between Spain, Cuba and North America.

On the corner of Tacón and San Ignacio, the religious building forms a point, leading us to the left along San Ignacio to Plaza de la Catedral. Before we reach this square, however, we can see the original portal on the corner with Calle Tejadillo. This is a typical baroque work with a certain Churrigueresque air dating to the 18th century. The portal forms part of the Cathedral, to which the Seminary is linked by the common constructive elements resulting from the original project drawn up by the Jesuits. Inside is a lovely stone porticoed cloister around a central patio, a monumental broad staircase in stone from San Miguel and heavy mahogany bannisters, as well as a fine wooden gate communicating with the upper floor.

Continuing along Calle San Ignacio, we come to the paved area of **Plaza de la Catedral (48)** which bustles with animation, just as it always has, with the continuous arrival of visitors from all over the world and the offer of an infinity of souvenirs and art and craft objects, paintings and wooden carvings inspired in the characters and legends of Afro-Cuban mythology and folklore. Nothing would lead us to think that four centuries ago this square was an unhealthy swamp, impossible to pass through, where a spring, serving as a cattle watering place and a source of water supply for ships.

The first thing to be built on this site in around 1587 was a cistern to store the water from its natural springs. Later, over the years, the land was dried and the first houses were built. In 1623, before the cathedral was built, this square was known as Plaza de la Ciénaga ("Swamp Square"). In the 18th century, the frays of the Company of Jesus bought a piece of land in the north side of the square and began to lay the first stones of what was to be the Oratory of San Ignacio.

In 1767, with the college almost completed and the church still unfinished, the Jesuits were expelled from the country, as well as from Spain and its other dominions, at the order of King Charles III. In 1772, in view of the ruinous, dangerous state of the old Parroquial Mayor Church opposite Plaza de Armas, it was decided to transfer it to the church of the Jesuits, an act which was carried out with great solemnity on 9 November 1772.

By order of Bishop Felipe José de Trespalacios, in 1788 work began on the and transformation of what was then the Oratorio of San Ignacio into a **Cathedral** devoted to the **Immaculate Conception (49),** a statue of whom is installed at the High Altar. During the bishopric of José Díaz de Espada and Fernández de Landa, in the early-19th century, the Cathedral underwent further alteration, with the replacement of all that which the bishop considered in poor taste by copies of works by Rubens, Murillo and other great masters, painted by Juan Bautista Vermay.

The church forms a rectangle divided into a nave and two aisles by great

House of the Count of Bayona. Colonial Art Museum.

Craftwork in the Plaza de la Cathedral.

pillars and eight side chapels. Of these, the oldest is the Chapel of Nuestra Señora de Loreto, consecrated by Bishop Morell de Santa Cruz in 1755, before the transformation of the Oratory into the Cathedral. The author of the project for the church stayed anonymous, though it is believed to have been one of the Jesuits, judging by the character of the building and its architectural unity. The front is attributed to Pedro Medina of Cadiz, who also worked on the Palace of the Captains General.

The sculptures and fine silver work of the high altar and its tabernacle, in rich marble and precious metals are the work of the Italian artist Bianchini, who completed them in Rome in 1820. Behind the high altar are three large original frescoes by the renowned painter Giusseppe Perovani. These and the paintings by Vermay are the most notable works in the Cathedral.

Until the end of Spanish domination of Cuba, the nave featured an imposing funeral monument erected in commemoration of Christopher Columbus and which was said to contain the ashes of the *Gran Almirante*. In 1898, the monument and the remains were transferred to Seville Cathedral, where they are to this day. Nevertheless, the cathedral contains many other interesting tombs, particularly, in the Chapel of Loreto, that of Bishop Apolinar Serrano, over which is a statue of him at prayer.

The Cathedral is the maximum exponent of what has become known as "Cuban baroque", a style whose main canons are amply illustrated in the front of the building. One of the great enigmas of the Cathedral lies in the difference in size of the two towers, for the right-hand tower is wider than that on the left, something which responds to no logic of construction unless it was done in order to leave space for Calle San Ignacio.

The most attractive of the images in the Cathedral is that of Saint Christopher, a wooden statue carved by Martín Andujar in Seville and which was brought to Havana in 1633 for installation in the Parroquial Mayor Church. Composed over 170 pieces, the work was so large that in order to make it easier to carry in processions, a sculptor was commissioned to reduce its size. As a result of this, though the work was carried out relatively well, there is a noticeable disproportion between the head and the body. Saint Christopher is the patron saint of Havana. Plaza de la Catedral was the square chosen for the residence of illustrious and powerful Havanan families who built noble mansions in accordance with their rich lineage. The carved stone of these outstanding buildings closes off the perimeter of the square.

The **House of the Counts of Casa Bayona,** opposite the Cathedral at the

La Bodeguita del Medio.

Calle Empedrado.

end of the square, is a charming rambling old house which at first glimpse may appear more hermetic than its companions, perhaps because it is the only one without porticoes. Inside are delightful apartments, closed shadowy patios and open galleries full of sun or moonlight. The house was built earlier than the Cathedral, in 1720, by Luis Chacón, a descendent of the counts of Casa Bayona who lend their name to the building. In the early-19th century it was acquired by the College of Scribes, greatly increasing the activity in the square. Later on, the newspaper La Discusión was published here. Now its rooms contain the collections of the Museum of Colonial Art, featuring a representative sample of the decoration and furnishings of the great mansions of the 18th and 19th centuries.

At the right-hand side of the square as we face the Cathedral are another two adjoining mansions of great interest. In 1741, the Royal Treasurer, Don Diego Peñalver y Angulo built his sumptuous residence here. His son, Ignacio Peñalver, named Marquis of Arcos for his services during the English siege and occupation of Havana, resided in it, as did his descendants who, in the mid-19th leased it to the post office administration. The **House of the Marquis of Arcos** has two fronts, one giving onto the square and the other onto Calle Mercaderes, the latter being the main front. The building is a perfect example of the colonial house, particularly notable in its staircase and hallway. It has porticoes overlooking the square with five arcades on Doric columns. Its balcony is richly decorated.

The **House of the Marquis of Lombillo** stands at the corner of the square with Calle Empedrado and also has two fronts. The building was

House of the Count of Lombillo.

completed in 1741 and was extended in 1746 when the porticoes were added. Its owner then was José de Pedroso y González. In 1874, the sugar trading company San Gabriel had its offices here. This company was the property of the third Count of Lombillo, who resided in the house and was married to one of the Pedroso family. In 1937, it was the seat of the National Defence Secretariat, and it was later occupied by various official institutions. It now houses the Education Museum.

The **House of the Marquises of Aguas Claras** stands on the opposite side of the square. It is presently occupied by the Restaurant "El Patio", which specialises in Cuban and international cuisine. It has a central courtyard with a fountain providing a fresh, relaxing atmosphere amidst ornamental vegetation. The mansion dates to the 18th century and belonged to Francisco Filomeno Ponce de León, third Marquis of Aguas Claras. In 1870 it was sold to the Counts of San Fernando de Peñalver, and it is known by both titles.

The house on the side leading into **Callejón del Chorro** formerly housed the first public baths in Havana, established in around 1840. The baths took their water supply from the spring in the square, using the old Zanja Real canal. It is now the art shop of the Cuban Cultural Heritage.

At the corner of this house with San Ignacio and Callejón del Chorro is a plaque commemorating the canal which supplied Havana with water for over 250 years reached as far as Plaza de la Cathedral. El Callejón del Chorro was formerly known as Callejón del

Jagüey, and was completely covered as far as Calle Monserrate. The water from the Zanja came from a point on the River Almendares, a distance of more than ten kilometres away, to the square. The Zanja Real was completed in 1592 after fifty years' work, remaining in service until the mid-19th century.

We shall terminate this extensive itinerary at that sanctuary of rum but, above all, restaurant serving the finest Creole cuisine, that is the Bodeguita del Medio, entering from Calle Empedrado by the side of the Cathedral leading to San Ignacio. There is no place in the world like this, so Bohemian, so centrally-located and so nostalgic, its walls plastered with illustrious signatures and anonymous graffitis, so full of people and at the same time so personal. The **Bodeguita del Medio (50)** was founded by Ángel Martínez, a Spanish immigrant with a special talent for business who arrived here in the 1930s. His establishment soon became a favourite amongst Cuban intellectuals, attracted to it by its cheerful atmosphere, excellent food and that sensational cocktail, the Mojito, a veritable conspiracy between rum and mint. Those who have sat at these tables include such celebrities as Rocky Marciano, Gary Cooper, Spencer Tracy, Marlene Dietrich, Luis Miguel Domínguín and many, many more.

Once we have delighted our palates with a veritable festival of pork, *congrí* and *plátanos tostones,* we can make our way back via San Ignacio, taking Calle Obispo once more to return to our starting-point in Central Park.

Fortress of San Carlos de La Cabaña, seen from Avenida del Puerto.

ITINERARY V

ITINERARY NUMBER FIVE:

51- Hotel Plaza.
52- Museum of the Revolution and Granma Memorial.
53- Church of El Santo Angel Custodio.
54- National Music Museum.
55- Bay Tunnel.
56- Palace of Mateo Pedroso.
57- Castle of San Salvador de la Punta.
58- Martyrs' Park (Parque de los Mártires).
59- Monument to the Eight Medical Students.
60- Monument to General-in-Chief Máximo Gómez.
61- Hotel Sevilla.

The **Hotel Plaza (51),** a veritable classic amongst Havanan hotels, is our starting-point for this fifth itinerary. It first opened its doors on 29 December 1908, and has maintained its charming, romantic, 19th-century air intact to this very day.

Setting off under the broad arcades of the Plaza which lead to Calle Neptuno, we come to Monserrate, opposite Supervielle Park. Here is a bust commemorating Dr. Manuel Fernández Supervielle, mayor of Havana during the 1940s. The doctor's principal electoral promise was to resolve the city's water supply problem, as water was scarce due to the high growthrate. Time passed, and the promise was not kept due to the failure of central government to transfer the funds due to the city. Months after being sworn in, the mayor committed suicide, and it was said that it was the shame caused by his failure to keep his promise which had led him to the fatal decision. Paradoxically, less than one hundred metres from this monument is the statue of Albear, who built Havana's first aqueduct. Monserrate leads to Trocadero, where we find the **National Fine Arts Museum,** opposite the Granma Memorial, which forms part of the Museum of the Revolution .

At the moment this guide was written, the Fine Arts Museum was being completely reorganised, a task which should be completed in the next three years. The museum's main collections are devoted to Cuban art, with paintings from the 17th century to modern times, and European art, with originals by Murillo, Zurbarán, Velazquez, Goya, Hans Memling, Sorolla and others. The ancient art collection, containing Greek and Roman works, is considered the most important of its kind in Latin America.

At this point, the **Granma Memorial** is fully in view. This, as its name indicates, features the yacht Granma, the 20-metre vessel which brought Fidel Castro to Cuba from Mexico along with 81 revolutionary combatants. After seven days' arduous sailing, the Granma

Hotel Plaza.

Hotel Plaza. Interior.

reached the southern coastline of the eastern region of Cuba on 2 December 1956. After disembarking in swamplands, harried by national aircraft and ground fighters, Fidel and his men reached the mountains of the Sierra Maestra, unleashing the insurrection which was to culminate in victory on 1 January 1959. Around the yacht are arms and historic objects used in different events occurring during the revolutionary struggle, the Battle of Playa Girón and the missile crisis (known to the Cubans as the "October Crisis").

The **Museum of the Revolution (52)** is housed the what was the Presidential Palace from 1920 until the early-1960s. We reach the Granma Memorial by crossing the museum. The four-storey Presidential Palace was built entirely in finely-cut white stone, crowned by a lantern in the centre giving the building considerable height. The palace is built in a notably eclectic style. Opposite is Avenida de las Misiones, a broad thoroughfare leading up to the palace and commanding magnificent views of the bay entrance.

The interior contains a treasure-trove of marble, columns and high windows, vast salons, particularly the Mirror Room (Salón de los Espejos), a replica of that in Versailles, and the Gold Room (Salón Dorado), decorated with yellow marble. The paintings displayed are all of the finest quality and are by such Cubans artists of the period as Menocal, Romañach and Valderrama.

The Museum of the Revolution provides a complete vision, backed up by documents, photographs and many other objects, of the history of

Presidential Palace. Museum of the Revolution.

Mirror Room.

the struggles of the Cuban people for independence since the times of the Spanish colonists to the consolidation of the revolutionary process, notwithstanding the constant confrontation with the island's most power enemy, the United States. The museum also has a section devoted to the spectacular assault on the Presidential Palace by a commando of young revolutionaries on 13 March 1957 with the aim of putting an end to the life of the dictator, Fulgencio Batista, so as to speed up the victory of the armed insurrection. Batista managed to escape through a secret door in his office, however, frustrating an action in which most of the revolutionaries were killed.

Opposite the building is one of the sentry posts in the wall and, on a pedestal a SAU-100 Soviet-manufactured tank with which Fidel Castro opened fire on the Houston, one of the boats used to transport the mercenaries who disembarked at the Bay of Pigs in April 1961.

On leaving the museum, we head for the Church of **El Santo Angel Custodio (53),** attention caught by its white Gothic domes. We now take Calle Cuarteles to Calle Compostela, the street leading to the main entrance of the church, which was built in 1695 by Bishop Diego Evelino de Compostela. The building stands at the top of

Church of El Santo Angel Custodio.

the street which was later named after this bishop, on a hill then known as Peña Pobre, now Loma del Angel.

Founded as an auxiliary church for the Parroquial Mayor Church, the building was badly damaged by a strong hurricane in 1846. It was completely rebuilt the following year in the fine Gothic style which we can even now appreciate. The interior was also greatly embellished as part of the reconstruction work. Two illustrious sons of Havana were christened in the Church of El Santo Angel, Félix Varela and José Martí, and this was also the scene of the events of that great 19th-century novel by Cirilo Villaverde, "Cecilia Valdés". This sets the life of its heroin around the Loma del Ángel and the culminating scene outside the church entrance.

We now go down from the Loma del Angel, taking Calle Cuarteles. A block or two further on, we come to Calle Peña Pobre, where the crossroads of Calles Habana, Cuarteles and Espada form a strange junction known as Las Cinco Corner of El Ángel ("the five corners of the Angel"), surrounded by a particularly splendid colonial urban landscape. Some of the houses in these streets still have beams of round trunks which testify to their age.

At the junction of Peña Pobre and Habana, the latter street opens up to provide a broad perspective towards the Monument to Máximo Gómez, hero of Cuban independence, and Calle Tacón, where we find the delightful surprise, on the right, of the lovely little palace which houses the **National Music Museum (54),** with its structure of stone arches and columns. This museum, the only one of its kind in Cuba, provides an overview of the music and instruments of Cuba throughout history. There is also an excellent collection of original musical scores, old editions of documents relating to music, records, rare and curious instruments, books and art works. A visit to this museum takes us down the roads which made Cuban music the national element which has had the greatest influence on universal culture.

Facing us now is the entrance roundabout to the **Bay Tunnel (55),** whose 800-metre length connects the centre with the eastern outskirts of Havana by the Vía Monumental, which also leads to the city of Matanzas and from there to Varadero in a journey taking around one hour.

Continuing along the right-hand side of Calle Tacón, we come to the typically Havanan **Bar Cabaña.** This popular bar is full of life from mid-morning to well into the next day. The Bar Cabaña, with its 50s decor, serves a veritable delirium of rum, its happy customers dancing and listening to the juke box music for hours before finally driving off in their veteran cars to enjoy the breeze along El jetty, with no hurry and no particular place to go...

The Bar Cabaña, then, is ideal for the night, the evening or the day.

Music Museum.

Entrance to the Tunnel and monument to Máximo Gómez.

We, meanwhile, head for the sentry box of the seaboard strip of city walls less than one hundred metres away. The waves used to enter the port at this point, beating against this sentry box. Now, however, it is surrounded by terra firma as a result of the construction of the Avenida del Puerto. During the English conquest of Havana in 1762, this was the only stretch of wall to come into combat, fired on by English canons from the heights of La Cabaña and El Morro once these had given up all resistance. Before the wall was built here, the spot was known as Playa de las Tortugas due to the number of turtles found on the beach. Opposite is the **Palace of Mateo Pedroso (56),** in Calle Cuba between Cuarteles and Peña Pobre. Mateo Pedroso was governor and mayor of Havana. The building, which dates to 1780 has four floors including the mezzanine, with a monumental, austere front. It has a magnificent Moorish style running balcony, whilst the patio is surrounded by four wide galleries and is the most spacious of all those in the old city. Its robustness can be judged by the fact that stone from the same quarry was used to build La Cabaña Fortress. The building is now a large shopping and leisure centre.

A short distance away, the stonework of the castle of the former

Havana Police Department might lead us to believe that this is a work of historic importance, but it is not so. The castle is a pseudo-colonial construction dating to the year 1941, built using stone from the Maestranza de Artillería which was built in the 19th century and stood on this site until it was demolished.

We now cross the park and take the first street on the left, Calle Chacón, to come out in Avenida del Puerto. This, as we know, was built after a large section of the bay canal had been reclaimed. This is an ideal spot for a carefree stroll, enjoying the feeling of space, timelessness and warm sun, until we come to the buried cannons where the port chain was tied and the **Castle of San Salvador de la Punta (57).** In the far-off days of the 17th century, the port had a chain which closed it off from either side to prevent the entry of enemy ships. This chain was made up of several lines supported by thick wooden beams. The ends were attached to cannons embedded in the reefs on either side, El Pescante and La Punta.

The Castle of San Salvador de la Punta was built on an outcrop of land at the mouth of the entrance to the bay and always recognised for its strategic importance. Building began in 1589, at the same time as the Castle of Los Tres Reyes del Morro on the opposite side of the bay. The defensive system designed by the engineer Bautista Antonelli revolved around the idea of being able to provide crossfire from the gun batteries of the two fortresses. The castles were completed in 1600, and though modifications were later introduced, these always respected the basic original layout.

Peña Pobre.   *Hotel Sevilla.*

ITINERARY V

At La Punta, if we pause exactly opposite El Morro , we can see all around us one of the most beautiful views of Havana, breathtaking no matter how many times one has seen it.

On the other side of the avenue is the splendid, graceful statue of Máximo Gómez Baez, standing in the middle of the tunnel entrance roundabout. On the right, not far off, is **Martyrs' Park (58)** (Parque de los Mártires) and the **Monument to the Eight Medical Students.** The site now occupied by Martyrs' Park , delimited by El Prado, Capdevila (Tacón), Avenida del Puerto and tunnel entrance roundabout, formerly stood the Tacón Prison, built in 1838 by Captain General Don Miguel Tacón, famous for his implacable persecution of political conspirators and common criminals alike. Tacón's rise to power brought with it an immediate increase in the prison population, in response to which the Captain General undertook the construction of prison accommodation for over 2,000 inmates, divided into departments for different sexes, classes and types of offense. This penitentiary included amongst its inmates many political prisoners, often falsely accused of seditious activity, such as the Medical Students, eight of whom faced the firing squad. Others were persecuted for taking part in conspiracies from the mid-19th century onwards which aimed to free the island from Spanish domination. Amongst these patriots was José Martí, imprisoned for several months between 1869 and 1870. The execution ground lay in the esplanade of La Punta, between the prison and the castle, and it

House of Mateo Pedroso. Craft Palace.

Monument to Máximo Gómez.

was here that those condemned to die for political or common crimes were garrotted.

After the demolition of the prison in 1939, Martyrs' Park was built in memory of all those who suffered their for their ideals. Nevertheless, two of the punishment cells and the chapel where those condemned to die spent their final hours were conserved as reminders of that infamous institution.

The **Monument to the Eight Medical Students (59)** stands in the section of the park near to La Punta. The Templete commemorates the tragic, moving events caused by political intolerance during the 1970s and which terminated with the execution by firing squad of eight students from the medical faculty in Havana, accused of profaning the tomb of a Spanish journalist, infamous for his anti-Cuban stance, who had died in a duel with a Creole in the United States . The trial could not prove the guilt of the young men but outraged members of the Volunteer Corps forced the random selection of eight of the accused, one of whom was not even in the city on the day of the events for which they were being tried. The monument conserves the fragment of wall against which the students were shot.

In the middle of the tunnel entrance roundabout stands the **Monument to General-in-Chief Máximo Gómez (60),** at the beginning of Avenida de las Misiones, which leads up to the Presidential Palace, overlooking the bay. Gómez is portrayed in this statue bare-headed, looking up as he reins in his horse. By the Italian artist Aldo Gamba, the monument was inaugurated on 18 November 1935. It has three sections featuring various symbols relating to the Patria, the People and Freedom.

Máximo Gómez, General-in-Chief of the Army of Liberation, was born in Bani, Dominican Republic, in 1836. He placed his extraordinary military genius at the service of the cause of Cuban independence, instructing the leaders of the first stage of the ten-year war from 1868 to 1878. Designated by the Cuban Revolutionary Party created by José Martí, he then led the second stage of the armed struggle from 1895 to 1898, carrying out his mission with outstanding brilliance. He died in Havana on 17 June 1905.

After a pleasant stroll around the spacious esplanade of La Punta, its castle and monuments, the itinerary now takes us to Zulueta, where at the beginning of this street stands a building which attracts our attention not only because it is the seat of the Spanish Embassy in Cuba, but because it is the most interesting exponent of the Art Nouveau style, which became popular in Havana during the early decades of the 20th century. The building's original owner was a rich businessman, Dionisio Velasco, a member of the Sarrá family, which controlled the pharmaceutical business in Cuba.

Our tour ends at another of Havana's classical hotels, the **Hotel Sevilla (61),** where a touch of authentic Mudéjar style reminds us of how close the city of Guadalquivir is in tradition and culture to this city of columns and endless arcades in the tropics.

Monument on the spot where the Eight Medical Students were shot in 1871.

Martyrs' Park (Parque de los Mártires). Chapel of the former Tacón Prison. Castle of San Salvador de la Punta.

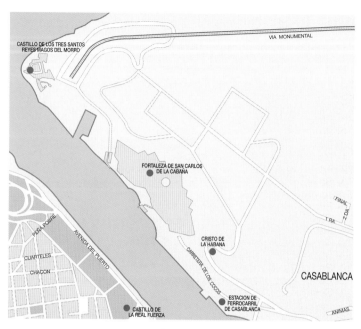

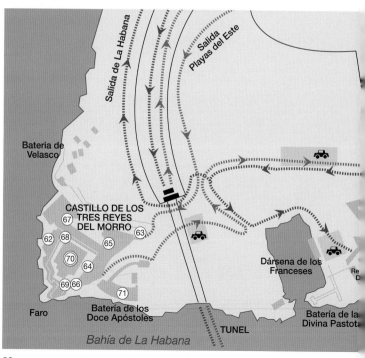

ITINERARY NUMBER SIX:

62- Castle of Los Tres Reyes del Morro .
63- Aspillerado Tunnel.
64- Camino de Ronda (Sentry Path).
65- Austria Bastion.
66- Semaphore Station.
67- Tejeda Bastion
68- Plataform of La Reina.
69- *Surtida de los Tinajones.*
70- Central Building.
71- Battery of Los "Doce Apóstoles".
72- Fortaleza de San Carlos de la Cabaña.
73- San Leopoldo Revellin.
74- *Tenaza de San Antonio.*
75- Plaza de Armas (Parade Ground).
76- Chapel.
77- Patio de los Jagüeyes.
78- Arms Development Room.
79- Moat of Los Laureles.
80- San Julián Revellin.
81- Calle de Marina.
82- Semibastion of San Lorenzo.
83- La Cortina (curtain wall).
84- Comandancia del Che.

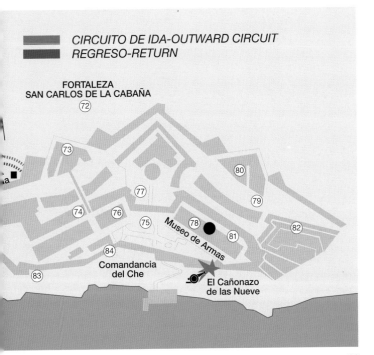

This itinerary takes us firstly through the tunnel to the eastern bank of the Bay of Havana. We can do this taxi to the Castle del Morro, or by *ciclobus,* a special bus line transporting cyclists and many more pedestrian passengers on each journey. This bus, or "guaguas", as the Havanans call it, starts out from Martyrs' Park (Parque de los Mártires) at La Punta. Once we emerge from the tunnel on the other side of the bay, we should get off at the first stop in La Cabaña and walk some 250 metres to the Castle of El Morro.

Our first surprise on arrival at the castle is the magnificent landscape we can observe from the *mirador* (belvedere) at the entrance, and in which the sea and the city combine in a unique, breathtaking view. We shall now begin a fascinating tour of the Morro-Cabaña Historic and Military Park, composed of the most powerful defensive complex built by the Spanish in America.

A relief, flat to the south and west and rising in the east, is the most significant characteristic of the Bay of Havana. Its heights extend from the hill at the canal entrance, stretching beyond the township of Casablanca. As early as the first half of the 16th century, the Havanans used El Morro as the site for lookout posts warning of the arrival of enemy ships. In 1563, Governor Diego de Mazariegos order the construction here of a brightly whitewashed tower extending the range of vision by over eight leagues and serving as a point of reference for galleons.

In April 1583, the Chapter installed El Morro fortress with the first six cannons, ordering that one at least of the lookouts on duty should know

Entrance to the Castle of Los Tres Reyes del Morro.

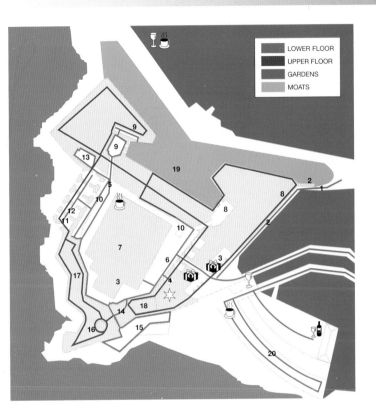

CASTLE OF LOS TRES REYES DEL MORRO

1 ENTRANCE
2 ASPILLERADO TUNNEL
3 ART GALLERY
4 SUB-AQUATIC ARCHAEOLOGY ROOM
5 GATE OF LA REINA PLATFORM
6 CAMINO DE RONDA (SENTRY PATH)
7 EXHIBITION ROOMS
8 AUSTRIA BASTION WITH CASEMENT
9 TEJEDA BASTION WITH CASEMENT
10 RAMPS
11 ACCESS TO THE UPPER FLOOR. (STAIRS)
12 HIGH AND LOW BATTERIES
13 LA REINA PLATFORM
14 LOS TINAJONES GATE
15 LA ESTRELLA PLATFORM
16 EL MORRO LIGHTHOUSE
17 EL MORRILLO HIGH BATTERY
18 SEMAPHORE STATION
19 MOATS
20 BATTERY OF LOS DOCE APOSTOLES
   "EL POLVORIN" BAR
   RESTAURANT "LOS DOCE APOSTOLES"
   CAFETERIA

El Morro Castle: Gallery of the Low Battery

Sentry Walk (Camino de Rondas).   *Curtain wall of the Austria Bastion.*

how to handle them. Moreover, a tiled sentry post was built to protect the sentries from bad weather.

In view of the growing danger which threatened the Town of San Cristobal de la Habana as it gained importance as the principal port in the Indies, of attacks by Corsairs and pirates or Spain's enemies, and the feeling that the Castle of La Real Fuerza was not sufficient to repel such attacks, persuaded King Philip II to approve the construction of a great fortress making the port impregnable. To this end, the engineer Juan Bautista Antonelli was commissioned, under the direction of the Captain General, Field Marshall Juan de Tejada, to undertake this work, which began in 1589.

The work is said to have had to overcome numerous difficulties caused by the constant shortage of workers and money, combined with the intrigues, complaints and disagreements of the engineer Antonelli with the Captains General. The castle was not finally finished until 40 years after the work began, during the times of Governor Lorenzo Cabrera. Alonso Sánchez Toro was appointed as its first warder, his wide-ranging powers including that of replacing the military governor of the island, the Captain General, in case of his death.

The **Castle of Los Tres Reyes del Morro (62)** forms an irregular polygon which follows perfectly the outline of the rocks on which it is built, and which form a considerable defensive asset. The stone from which it was built were cut *in situ*, extracted from the space forming the moats using rudimentary procedures requiring the use of hundreds of slaves.

The castle thrusts out towards the sea at a sharp angle, with a semi-bastion at this point over which is a beacon tower. From here to a depth of 150 metres, curtains open up successively until the rear side is reached, communicating with the land, protected by two solid bastions and a deep moat.

El Morro was the port of Havana's main defence until the construction of La Cabaña in the last third of the 18th century. For over a century it repelled the repeated assaults of Dutch, French and English fleets, in 1762 withstanding for 44 days the siege laid by Admiral Pocock's fleet, the most powerful in the Indies at that time. Throughout their history, the fortresses of the Morro-Cabaña Historic and Military Park have received the admiration of writers and travellers from different periods, and the Castle del Morro has become known all over the world as a representative symbol of the Island of Cuba.

To enter the castle, cross the wooden bridge and take the **Aspillerado Tunnel (63)** to the main gate. Originally, the entrance from the land was at a lower level, through a gate in the moat, but the castle communicated with the exterior principally by sea, via the Platform of La Estrella in the bay or the Platform of La Reina to the north.

Crossing the entrance gateway with its two thick wooden door, we find, on the right, the Cuban Cultural Heritage Collection Art

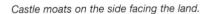

Castle moats on the side facing the land.

Semaphore Station.

Gallery, which both exhibits and sells art works, and, on the left, near the entrance to the parade ground, the souvenir shop.

The parade ground (Plazuela de Armas) really corresponds to the widest section of the **Camino de Rondas (64),** or castle sentry path, which joined all installations and dependencies in circular fashion.

Our itinerary is summarised in two sections, a visit to the upper part of the fortress, marked in blue on the map, and a tour of the lower area and the semi-bastion of the lighthouse and the high battery of El Morrillo, marked in red.

At the right-hand corner of the square is the entrance to the casement of the **Austria Bastion (65),** a covered area with loopholes overlooking the moats so that cannons could be installed. It was named in honour of the royal House of Austria, which ruled Spain during the period when the castle was built.

The ramp, paved with round pebbles, leads to the upper floor, where we find the Austria Bastion facing us on the right and the Tejeda Bastion on the left. From the steps by the wall, installed as sniper positions, is a panoramic view of the land around the castle. From the Austria Bastion, our view includes the exit from the Havana Tunnel, the Vía

Monumental and, in the background, the buildings of the Camilo Cienfuegos district in East Havana. Bordering the sea, we can observe an annex to the castle, the Velasco Battery, built in the 19th century as an extension to the exterior and coastal defensive system. The old stables here now house La Tasca, a tavern serving drinks and light meals. From the Austria Bastion, from the seaward side of the del Tejeda Bastion, we can make out the crevasse in the rock caused by the explosion of a mine placed by the English during the 44-day siege. A walk along the curtain wall shows the strategic relations between El Morro , La Cabaña (some 300 metres to the south), La Punta in the west, on the other side of the bay entrance, and La Fuerza, some one thousand metres into the bay canal. It is clear that, if we bear in mind the military tactics and weaponry of the 18th and 19th centuries, this defensive system was a formidable obstacle, and it is no surprise, therefore, that it was able to repel and dissuade attack for many years. Having enjoyed and appreciated this panorama, we can now visit the **Semaphore Station (66)** which has controlled the entrance and departure of shipping since 1888. The flagpole which stands nearby also has its own historical importance, as it was here that the flags legalising changes in the political status of the island were raised.

In the 18th century, the English flag was raised here once all resistance from the castle had been quashed, but the Spanish flag replaced it once more one year later, when Havana came under its rule again. In 1899, when Spain finally lost control of Cuba, its flag

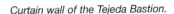

Curtain wall of the Tejeda Bastion.

Niches in the Sentry Walk.

was struck for the last time, replaced by that of the United States, which began its military occupation of the island. On 20 May 1902, date of the creation of the Cuban Republic, the US colours gave way to the flag with its single star, raised in the midst of the struggle for independence, where it flew at the gallop over the field of battle.

During the 18th and 19th centuries, the fortress flagpole, visible from the port zone, was used to signal by semaphore the approach of boats, their number, type and identity, as well as the direction from which they came. These signals were repeated by the Castle of La Fuerza to inform the people and the fortress garrisons. This information is relayed even today, broadcast by specialists and port pilots. On public holidays, the beautiful tradition of adorning the flagpole with the multicoloured signals flags is still continued. Amongst them, an enormous Cuban flag stands out, reaffirming the sovereignty of the island and filling the Havanans with understandable pride.

Retracing our steps, we now head for the other side of the castle, overlooking the sea, over the **Tejeda Bastion (67)**. Its name was given to it by the Field Marshall who began work on El Morro as governor. At the bastion, we can see plaques commemorating the taking of Havana by the English. One, dating to 1879 and installed during the third stage of the reconstruction of El Morro , exalts the bravery of Navy Captain Luis de Velasco, who led the castle resistance. Another, placed by the British Embassy, commemorates the historic events in which the Royal Navy took part, whilst a third, laid by the mayor of the Spanish town of Noja, where Velasco was born, pays homage to his illustrious compatriot.

It was here that the final action of the British siege took place, beginning on 6 June 1762. On that day, a formidable fleet of 28 ships of the line and 145 transport ships reached Havana, crewed by 10,000 men and transporting 14,000 infantrymen and 4,000 African slaves as auxiliaries. The fleet and naval operations were commanded by Admiral Sir George Pocock, a veteran of innumerable combats, whilst the supreme chief of the of the invading forces and supreme commander of the entire expedition was George Keppel, Count of Albemarle, a personage with more influence at court than military prowess.

The siege of El Morro began in earnest on 1 de Julio, when the English troops, having completed the arduous task of entrenching in difficult conditions on the ground, were able to cover the fortress with their artillery. That day, a simultaneous attack was launched by land and sea, converting El Morro into a veritable hell of shrapnel, explosion and death which did not let up until the final assault on 30 July. Captain Luis de Velasco having known since the previous day that due to the exhaustion of his men and the many lost or wounded, as well as that fact that guns and ammunition were quickly running out, with the hill of La Cabaña taken and no hope of help from that direction, sent an emissary to his chiefs in the city to ask whether he should retire whilst it was still possible to do so across the bay, saving his men, or whether he should fight to the end. The reply

Platform of La Estrella.

Surtida de Tinajones.

was vague and confused, leaving Velasco's military honour only one option, that of holding out until the bitter end.

Albemarle, for his part, needed North American reinforcements in order to make the final attack, as the long siege in the intense heat, and disease, had seriously undermined his troops' fighting morale, putting more men out of action than the fighting itself.

At 2 o'clock in the afternoon of 30 June, a mine placed in a 70-foot deep gully exploded, opening up a breach in the Caballero del Mar, at the Tejeda Bastion, and the English troops rapidly launched a massive attack. Taken by surprise, the defensive forces barely had time to man the walls. Velasco was seriously wounded in the chest early on, and could do little to organise the defence. Marquis Gonzalez was literally blown to pieces along with the brave soldiers defending the flag. The entire fortress fell into British hands in less than a quarter of an hour. As a result of the fall of El Morro, the city of Havana surrendered on 13 August 1762.

Leaving the Tejeda Bastion, we turn left along the edge of the High Battery, overlooking the sea, to find the steps leading down to the lower floor, emerging on the platform of the High Battery of Morrillo, slightly elevated above the level of the Sentry Walk, going down the ramp on the left.

The ramp doorway leads into the so-called Batería Baja (Low Battery), which has six loopholes open towards the sea. Next, returning towards the Sentry Walk, we come out at the **Platform of La Reina (68),** one of the service entries to the castle, from which it received provisions by sea. A sombre legend hangs over this place: it is said that during the first decades of the century, when the castle was used as a prison, the guards used to challenge prisoners to jump into the sea by leaving the gate open. But in those days the bay was infested with sharks, and any attempted escape invariably ended in the jaws of one of those fearsome denizens of the deep. To the right of the exit is the entrance to the Casement of the Tejada Bastion, with loopholes for two cannons and a secret door so that its defenders could receive supplies from the external battlements.

The Sentry Path next leads us to the **Surtida de los Tinajones (69),** where rapeseed oil was kept in the 19th century as fuel for the lighthouse. From here, we can observe the original site of the Battery of Los Doce Apóstoles (of the Twelve Apostles), which commanded entrance to the bay practically from the height of the ships' rigging.

Our next port of call is the **lighthouse,** reached by a small ramp over the *surtida.* The lighthouse is 15 metres in height, its flashes of light reaching a distance of 18 miles every 15 seconds. The present tower was inaugurated in 1844 by the then Captain General,

Main building.

Ventanales.

Patio of Los Jagüeyes.

Leopoldo O'Donnell. Before and after the conquest of Havana by the English, the original lighthouse was fuelled by wood. In 1795 an unsuccessful attempt was made to use inflammable gas produced from Cuban *chapapote*. Oil began to be used in 1819 and, after 1845 rapeseed oil; in 1928, acetylene began to be used, and the lighthouse was finally installed with electrical lighting in 1945. This site is now a magnificent *mirador* (viewpoint).

Leaving the lighthouse, we retrace our steps to the parade ground to visit the **Central Building (70).** This building did not exist in the 17th century, instead there were seven independent buildings which functioned as the officers' mess, church, stores, barracks for the troops and other military and administrative dependencies. It had two large cisterns which could supply the garrison of one thousand men with water for a long period of time should the fortress become cut off.

As part of the reconstruction of the fortress in 1763, an enterprise carried out by engineers Silvestre Abarca and Agustín Cramer, these independent buildings were replaced by the central casemented construction we now see before us. Inside, the galleries are now devoted to permanent and temporary exhibitions. Currently, one permanent exhibition is devoted to the Great Voyages, illustrating the most important maritime expeditions undertaken by Spain and Portugal in the 15th and 16th centuries, broadening humanity's knowledge of the world.

The other permanent exhibition takes the form of the Underwater Archaeology Room, which displays objects recovered from the bottom of the Bay of Havana by underwater archaeological expeditions. Amongst the items forming part of the exhibition, the most interesting are those recovered from the cruiser Sánchez Barcáiztegui, which collided with the Mortera and sank at the bay entrance in the 19th century, and from the North American battleship Maine, which exploded in the bay in mysterious circumstances towards the end of the War of Independence, giving the United States the pretext they were looking for to step into the war, taking advantage of the inroads made by the Cubans over almost 30 years of struggle.

A tour of the exterior areas of the Castle of El Morro takes us unfailingly to visit the **Battery of Los Doce Apóstoles (71),** or Battery of the Sun, where the main restaurant facilities are also to be found. Leaving through the main doorway, we go down a long ramp, turning into the Camino del Polvorín to reach this 19th-century battery of cannons.

As far as refreshments are concerned, the visitor can choose between the bar "El Polvorín" ("the Powderhouse", where the gunpowder store really was), the "Batería del Sol" cafeteria or the restaurant "Los Doce Apóstoles", serving Cuban and international cuisine. Another establishment in the environs of El Morro and La Cabaña and well worth a worth a visit is the restaurant "La Divina Pastora", a charming place near the jetty with an excellent Creole and inter-

Parade ground, La Cabaña.

Panoramic view of the Moat of Los Laureles

national menu. Follow the path marked on the map to find this restaurant, as it is separate from the fortress site.

Our next visit is to the **Fortress of San Carlos de La Cabaña (72).** This was built at the command of King Charles III when he recovered rule over Havana as a result of the peace treaty with England signed in 1763.

Work began on 4 November 1763 and was completed eleven years later in 1774 at a cost of 14 million "duros". It is said that King Charles, when told of the enormous cost of the fortress, asked for a telescope so that he could "see such an enormous construction from Madrid..." The fortress was given the name of San Carlos in honour of the Spanish monarch.

La Cabaña, 700 metres in length and covering an area of ten hectares was without doubt the largest fortress built in the New World by Spain. It enjoyed a magnificent strategic position overlooking the city of Havana from a great balcony, with the bay canal on the one side and the sea to the north on the other. It has an inner polygon with bastions, terraces, chicken coops and flanked ravelins, and is surrounded by a deep moat cut into the rock, and a covered path with two slopes down to the shores of the bay. Its constructions include rude barracks and storehouses. The fortress was installed with powerful artillery from the very beginning, and its defensive weaponry was always kept ready for action at any time. In 1859 it had 120 bronze cannons and mortars and a garrison of 1,300 soldiers, which could be increased to six thousand when necessary. It was never attacked, however, and it is said that its dissuasive presence won all potential battles.

In the absence of glorious exploits or heroic actions, during the Wars of Independence the Fortress of La Cabaña served as a prison and site of executions. Its dungeons and moats were bore dumb witness to multiple assassinations of Cuban patriots. After the installation of the Republic, the fortress continued to be the unspoken-of scene of numerous political crimes during the governments of Machado and Batista.

After the triumph of the Revolution in January 1959, the fortress was occupied by the guerrilla forces of *Comandante* Ernesto Che Guevara. Subsequently, courts martial and trials for crimes against the security of the revolutionary state were held in La Cabaña. After 1986, when restoration work was completed, the fortress was opened to the public as a historic and military museum attraction.

Continuing our visit to San Carlos de la Cabaña, we now cross the covered path of the **San Leopoldo Revellin (73),** coming out at the **San Antonio Tenail (74).** These two structures were designed as advanced defensive obstacles which would put up a strong resistance against attack, strongly-manned and equipped with cannons.

Calle de la Marina.

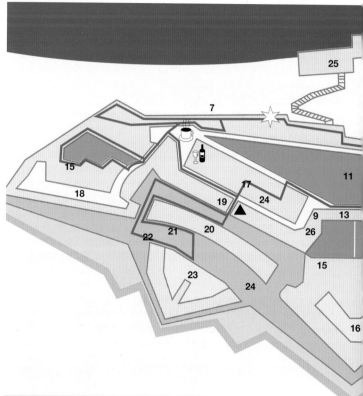

1 ENTRANCE.
2 SAN LEOPOLDO RAVELIN.
3 SAN ANTONIO TENAILLE.
4 SAN FRANCISCO SEMI-BASTION.
5 SAN JOSE PLATFORM.
6 LA PASTORA HIGH BATTERY.
7 CORTINA (CURTAIN WALL).
8 COMANDANCIA DEL CHE MEMORIAL MUSEUM.
9 ADMINISTRATIVE AREAS.
10 CHAPEL OF SAN CARLOS.
11 PARADE GROUND (PLAZA DE ARMAS).
12 OBELISK.
13 MONOGRAPHY OF THE FORTRESS.
14 CORTADURA (PATIO DE LOS JAGÜEYES).
15 MINE GALLERY.
16 SAN AMBROSIO BASTION.
17 ARMS AND FORTIFICATION MUSEUM.
18 SAN LORENZO SEMI-BASTION.
19 MOAT GATE.
20 SAN AGUSTIN TENAILLE.
21 PLAQUE COMMEMORATING THE EXECUTION
   OF CUBAN NATIONALISTS.
22 CENOTAPH OF JUAN CLEMENTE ZENEA.
23 SAN JULIAN RAVELIN.
24 CALLE DE MARINA.
25 JETTY.
26 TOILETS.
 🍷 WINE CELLAR.
 🛍 SHOPS.
 ☕ CAFETERIA.
 ☆ CEREMONY OF THE NINE O'CLOCK GUN.
 ► LA TIRADA. (CIGAR SHOP).

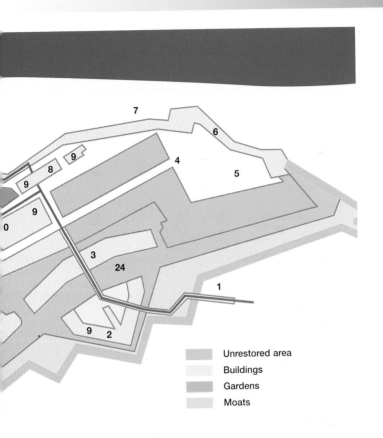

Unrestored area
Buildings
Gardens
Moats

Entrance to the Fortress of San Carlos de la Cabaña.

Havana, seen from the Semibastion of San Lorenzo.

The richness of the interior spaces of the fortress begins to become apparent with our first view of the monumental portal, flanked by great columns adjoining the pediment in which is the finely-carved escutcheon of King Charles III and a plaque dedicated to the engineers Silvestre Abarca and Pedro Medina, who directed the construction of the fortress, as well as the various governors who held command over the island at the time. It is said that the work was carried out in accordance with plans drawn up by the French engineer de Valliere and that the fortress was designed by another Frenchman, Ricaud de Tirgole.

Crossing another covered passage, a paved alley leads to the parade ground, or **Plaza de Armas (75),** with its 400 metres of curtain walls, buildings, bastions and gardens. Our attention is quickly drawn to the left, where we can see the **Chapel (76)** with its beautiful baroque front and a spire which serves as its belltower. During the restoration of this chapel, various burial places dating back to the 18th century were found, among them that of an officer of the artillery corps and those of women and children, indicating that the soldiers lived here with their families. The altar belonged to the now-lost Church of Santa Catalina and is fully in the style of the period, beautifully-carved in wood cut in the mountains near the city. The soldiery of La Cabaña particularly venerated three Catholic saints: Saint Charles, patron saint of the fortress, Saint Barbera, patron saint of artillerymen and Our Lady of El Pilar, patron saint of sailors.

In the adjoining building are craft and souvenir shops, an exhibition room pertaining to the Cultural Heritage Collection in which art works are displayed, and the **Monographic Exhibition** relating the history of the fortress through various objects, documents and photos. In the first section is a representation of the Ceremony of the Nine O'clock Cannon, with the uniforms and weapons corresponding to the three corps of the Spanish army, the infantry, the artillery and the cavalry. In an adjoining room is an exhibition referring to the obscure period when La Cabaña was a place of execution and a prison for those accused of political crimes. It includes a replica of the contraption used to garrotte those condemned to death, as well as various instruments of torture.

Adjoining the Monographic room is the entrance to the **Patio of Los Jagüeyes (77),** now a charming gardened spot but originally designed by the engineers in accordance with Renaissance military tactics, to be a serious obstacle for any enemy managing to overcome the other defenses. The *Cortadura,* as this defensive element is known in military language, could be packed with a powerful mine which would be exploded to prevent the entry of the enemy. The next building, which forms a long series of galleries stretching

Curtain wall, Fortress of La Cabaña.

Command post of Ernesto "Che" Guevara.

some 100 metres, takes us to the **rooms devoted to the development of weaponry (78)** from the primitive community up to the 17th century. The first room is devoted to the primitive community and the Ancient world (Greece and Rome). One of the principal exhibits is the full-scale model of a battering ram and a catapult. We might say that the catapult was a neuroballistic weapon, as it operated thanks to tensed animal nerves, whilst the battering ram was a weapon used for breaking down defenses.

The room devoted to the Middle Ages is the most complete, with a wide range of exhibits, including armour, axes, spears, crossbows and the formidable double-handed swords, the largest of all time. The room also contains a model of a medieval castle.

The exhibition on Modern Fortifications illustrates the Italian, German and French schools whose different influences helped to define the Latin American school. This room contains a model of a modern fortress and a large model featuring all the fortifications in Havana from the 16th century to the 19th.

The meeting of the two cultures through weaponry is the theme developed in the next room, which contains a collection of the rudimentary arms of the aboriginal population and those used by the Europeans during the conquest and colonisation of America.

A further two rooms present the great project for military construction by which Spain planned to fortify its main ports in America. Particular emphasis is placed on the project drawn up by the engineer Bautista Antonelli in Cuba.

This museum also contains a special exhibition of Japanese Katanas, the most perfect of all weapons of their type, curved Arabian scimitars, their scabbards beautifully adorned, and the fearsome Indian Katar with its three lacerating blades; and the so-called tiger claws, capable of causing dreadful wounds in imitation of the tiger's strike. This was a weapon much-feared by the British in India. We can now take the entrance to the **Moat of Los Laureles (79)** to visit the place used for executions, skirting the Tenaza of San Agustín on the right.

It is not known exactly how many people were executed in the Moat of Los Laureles, but the figure is thought to be well over one hundred. A large plaque commemorates the martyrdom suffered by those shot here, opposite which is a cenotaph marking the spot where the poet Juan Clemente Zenea was executed on 25 August 1871 for having put his pen to the service of the cause of freedom for Cuba.

Not far from here, in the **San Julián Revellin (80),** can now be seen for the first time the different types of ballistic weapons installed in Cuba during the so-called Missile Crisis, known to the Cubans as the

The Nine O'clock Cannon.

18th-century ceremonial cannon.

October 1962 Crisis. Here is a Soviet R-12 nuclear rocket with a range of 2, 500 kilometres, adapted to reduce its range of action to 2,000 kilometres to restrict it to only the possible confrontation with the United States. In all, 36 of these rockets were installed, along with anti-aircraft rocket, naval and terrestrial systems, of which there are models here. The October Crisis was one of the most difficult moments ever faced by the Cuban people and humanity in general, placing the world on the edge of a nuclear catastrophe. The R-12 rockets carried nuclear bombs whose destructive power was superior to those dropped on Hiroshima and Nagasaki.

Retracing our steps, we come out at the **Calle Marina (81).** To the left are the condemned cells, so that this was the last path trodden by those being taken to face the firing squad or garrotte. Opposite were the soldiers' barracks and equipment stores and ammunition dumps. We now turn at the southernmost end of the Plaza de Armas, where we see the Bodegón de los Vinos which, as its name indicates, centres its activity on that noble drink, wine. Crossing the little square in front of the old bakery, we cross a covered path to come out at the **Semi-bastion of San Lorenzo (82),** where the *caballero* of the semi-bastion stands out with the entire original artillery emplacement. This spot, on the border of La Cabaña with the Hill of Casablanca, is also where the mine galleries open up. The site commands beautiful views of the statue of El Cristo de Havana and of the bay, right out to its furthest points.

We now turn back to the curtain wall **La Cortina (83),** which extends almost 200 metres parallel to the canal. From here we can understand perfectly the strategic position of the fortress with regard to the city of Havana, and what it would have meant in the times the castle was in use for the enemy to command these heights. Lining the curtain wall is the battery of 18th-century ceremonial cannons. Each night, a picturesque military fantasy is performed here, with the orders of the old Spanish army ringing out, the cannon being readied and the boom as it is fired at nine o'clock, just as it did to warn that the city gates were closing. This ceremony is now one of the chief tourist attractions of the Morro-Cabaña Historic and Military Park.

Following the curtain wall, on the left is the obelisk erected in memory of the Spanish soldiers who died fighting against the separatist expedition led by Narciso López, in Cárdenas, on 19 May 1850. Under this monument is a crypt which once contained the ashes of these soldiers. Our final port of call on this tour of San Carlos de la Cabaña is the **Comandancia del Che (84).** This building contained the command post of guerrilla leader Ernesto "Che" Guevara, who entered the fortress on 3 January 1959, after the successful campaign in the centre of the island, where he had faced Fulgencio Batista's crack forces. Che summarises for Cubans the highest qualities of man and the revolutionary.

18th-century ceremonial cannon.

DIRECTORY OF OLD HAVANA

HOTELS:
Hotel Santa Isabel
Calle Baratillo number 9 between Obispo and Narciso López, Old Havana.
Tel: 33.82.01   fax: 33.83.91.
Hotel Ambos Mundos
Calle Obispo number 153 corner of Mercaderes, Havana Vieja.
Tel: 66.95.30   Fax: 66.95.32.
Hostal Valencia
Calle Oficios number 53 corner of Obrapía, Havana Vieja.
Hostal Condes de Villanueva
Calle Mercaderes number 202, corner of Lamparilla, Havana Vieja.
Hotel Inglaterra
Calle Paseo de Martí, between San Rafael and Neptuno. Old Havana.
Tels: 33.85.93 to 97   Fax: 33.82.54
Hotel Plaza
Calle Zulueta corner of Neptuno. Old Havana.
Tels: 33.85.83 al 90   Fax: 33.85.92 - 33.85.91.
Hotel Sevilla
Calle Trocadero between Paseo Martí and Zulueta. Old Havana.
Tels: 33.85.60 and 61.65.80   Fax: 33.85.82

RESTAURANTS:

El Patio (Bar restaurant, cafeteria)
Calle San Ignacio, corner of Empedrado, Plaza de la Cathedral, Havana Vieja.
Tels: 61.85.04 and 61.85.11.
Don Giovanni (bar restaurant, cafeteria)
Calle Tacón number 4, corner of Empedrado, Old Havana.
La Torre de Marfil (Restaurant)
Calle Mercaderes between Obispo and Obrapía. Tel: 62.34.66
La Zaragozana (Restaurant, bar, snack bar)
Calle Monserrate, number 352, between Obispo and Obrapía, Havana Vieja.
Cabaña (Bar restaurant)
Calle Cuba, number 12, corner of Peña Pobre, Havana Vieja.
Tel: 33.56.70
Al Medina (Restaurant cafeteria)
Calle Oficios number 12, between Obispo and Obrapía, Havana Vieja.
Tel: 63.08.62
Castillo de Farnés (restaurant bar)
Calle Monserrate, corner of Obrapía, Havana Vieja.
Tel: 63.12.60
La Mina (restaurant, snack bar, café)
Calle Obispo, corner of Oficios, Plaza de Armas, Havana Vieja.
Tel: 62.02.16

Hanoi (Restaurant)
Calle Teniente Rey, corner of Bernaza, Havana Vieja.
Tel: 63.16.81
Puerto de Sagua (Restaurant, snack bar)
Calle Egido number 603, between Jesús María and Acosta, Havana Vieja.
Tel: 63.61.86
La Bodeguita del Medio (Restaurant bar)
Calle Empedrado, between San Ignacio and Mercaderes, Havana Vieja.
Tel: 61.84.42
El Floridita (Bar restaurant)
Calle Monserrate corner of Obispo, Havana Vieja.
Tel: 63.10.63

CAFETERIAS

El Mercurio
Lonja del Comercio, Plaza de San Francisco de Asís, Havana Vieja.
Café París
Calle San Ignacio, corner of Obispo.
Bar Monserrate
Calle Monserrate, corner of Obrapía.
Bar Dos Hermanos / Two Brothers Bar
Avenida del Puerto, corner of Santa Clara, Havana Vieja.
Café O'Reilly
Calle O'Reilly, number 203, between San Ignacio and Cuba, Havana Vieja.
La Marina
Calle Teniente Rey corner of Oficios, Havana Vieja.
La Lluvia de Oro
Calle Obispo, corner of Habana, Havana Vieja.
La Casa de las Infusiones
Calle Mercaderes number 109, corner of Obispo, Havana Vieja.
El Juvenil
Calle Monte, corner of Cienfuegos, Havana Vieja.
Los Marinos
Calle Egido, corner of Merced, Havana Vieja.
Torrelavega
Calle Obrapía, between Mercaderes and Oficios, Havana Vieja.

IN THE OPEN AIR

Feria Fornos
Calle Neptuno and San Miguel, centro Habana.
La Torre de Oro
Calle Tacón corner of Empedrado, Havana Vieja.
La Casablanca
Calle Empedrado, between Tacón and Avenida del Puerto. Havana Vieja.

Doña Isabel
Calle Empedrado, corner of Tacón. Havana Vieja.
Isamán
Avenida del Puerto, corner of Empedrado, Havana Vieja.
Heladería (Ice-creams)
Calle Tacón, corner of Empedrado, Havana Vieja
Los Cañones
Calle Cuba, corner of Peña Pobre, Havana Vieja.
El Paso
Calle San Rafael, between Zulueta and Monserrate, Havana Vieja.
El Bosquecito
Calle San Ignacio, corner of O'Reilly, Havana Vieja.
La Punta
Ave. del Puerto, Castle de la Punta, Havana Vieja.

MARKETS

Cuatro Caminos
Calle Monte, between Matadero and Manglar, Havana Vieja.
Avenida del Puerto
Oficios number 406, between Luz and Acosta, Havana Vieja.
El Morro
Calle Cárcel, between Morro and Prado, Havana Vieja.
Los Marinos
Calle Egido, corner of Merced, Havana Vieja.
Belén
Compostela number 759, between Jesús María and Merced, Havana Vieja.
Cristo
Calle Teniente Rey number 461, between Bernaza and Cristo. Havana Vieja.
Fornos
Neptuno and San Miguel, Centro Habana.

SHOPS

El Clip (clocks, watches and jewellery)
Calle Obispo number 521 between Villegas and Bernaza. Old Havana.
Salón Crusellas (perfumes and silk good)
Calle Obispo number 522 between Villegas and Bernaza. Havana Vieja.
La Sorpresa (childrenswear)
Calle Obispo number 520, between Villegas and Bernaza. Havana Vieja.
La Inesita (furs and womenswear)
Calle Obispo number 508, between Villegas and Bernaza. Havana Vieja.
Clubman (menswear, perfumes and furs)
Calle Obispo number 514, between Villegas and Bernaza. Havana Vieja.

Humada (electronic goods and hardware)
Calle Obispo number 502, corner of Villegas.
Al Capricho (boutique and clothes)
Calle Obispo number 458 between Aguacate and Villegas. Old Havana.
La Francia (general store)
Calle Obispo number 452 corner of Aguacate. Old Havana.
Habana (boutique)
Calle Obispo number 415 corner ofguacate. Old Havana
Benetton (boutique)
Calle Oficios number 152 corner of Amargura, Plaza de San Francisco, Old Havana.
Langwith (gardening and pets' accessories)
Calle Obispo number 410, between Aguacate and Compostela. Old Havana.
Revert (boutique, household goods)
Calle Obispo number 403, corner of Compostela. Old Havana.
Topeka (toys and children's books)
Calle Obispo number 413, between Aguacate and Compostela. Old Havana.
Puerto Carenas (Cuban products)
Terminal del Crucero, Ave. del Puerto.

OTHERS

Cremería el Naranjal.
Calle Obispo corner of Cuba. Old Havana
Panadería San José (baker's)
Calle Obispo between San Ignacio and Mercaderes. Old Havana.

Useful telephone numbers

Ambulance
40.45.51 to 53
40.50.93 to 94
Cardiovascular Service:
40.71.73
Fire Brigade
81.11.15
Police
82.01.16
Taxi Services:
Panataxi:
81.30.08 / 81.30.65 /81.31.13 / 81.32.57 / 81.33.11.
Taxis Transgaviota:
20.44.55 / 20.46.50 / 33.97.00.
Taxis Transtur (Turistaxi):
33.55.41 / 33.55.42.

CONTENTS